RESILIENCE OF 100-YEAR FAMILY ENTERPRISES

How Opportunistic Innovation, Business Discipline, and a Culture of Stewardship Guide the Journey Across Generations

> *"You do not inherit a family business.*
> *You borrow it from your grandchildren."*
> – Hermes family descendent

WORKING PAPER BY DENNIS T. JAFFE, PH.D.

WISE COUNSEL RESEARCH
76 CANTON AVENUE
MILTON, MA 02186

DJAFFE@DENNISJAFFE.COM
DENNIS@WISECOUNSELRESEARCH.COM
WWW.WISECOUNSELRESEARCH.COM
WWW.DENNISJAFFE.COM

WORKING PAPER #5: 100 YEAR FAMILY RESEARCH PROJECT

THIS PAPER IS SPONSORED BY MERRILL LYNCH'S CENTER FOR FAMILY WEALTH DYNAMICS AND GOVERNANCE®, MERRILL LYNCH'S FAMILY OFFICE SERVICES AND U.S. TRUST, BANK OF AMERICA PRIVATE WEALTH MANAGEMENT

April, 2018

RESILIENCE OF 100-YEAR FAMILY ENTERPRISES

How Opportunistic Innovation, Business Discipline,
and a Culture of Stewardship
Guide the Journey Across Generations

*"You do not inherit a family business.
You borrow it from your grandchildren."*
– Hermes family descendent

WORKING PAPER BY DENNIS T. JAFFE, PH.D.

WISE COUNSEL RESEARCH
76 CANTON AVENUE
MILTON, MA 02186

DJAFFE@DENNISJAFFE.COM
DENNIS@WISECOUNSELRESEARCH.COM
WWW.WISECOUNSELRESEARCH.COM
WWW.DENNISJAFFE.COM

WORKING PAPER #5: 100 YEAR FAMILY RESEARCH PROJECT

THIS PAPER IS SPONSORED BY MERRILL LYNCH'S CENTER FOR FAMILY WEALTH DYNAMICS AND GOVERNANCE®, MERRILL LYNCH'S FAMILY OFFICE SERVICES AND U.S. TRUST, BANK OF AMERICA PRIVATE WEALTH MANAGEMENT

April, 2018

HOW OPPORTUNISTIC INNOVATION, BUSINESS DISCIPLINE, AND A CULTURE OF STEWARDSHIP
GUIDE THE JOURNEY ACROSS GENERATIONS

Contents

Part One – Uncovering the Wisdom of Multi-Generational Enterprising Families

Successful family enterprises are incredible engines for generating wealth and expressing the owning family's values about business and the community. These values may be expressed through the quality of their goods and services, relationships with employees, business and community, and philanthropy. But only a small fraction of the families that create businesses are able to sustain them for more than a single generation. The few surviving enterprises are huge and have a powerful impact on the community, global commerce, and the environment. They also have a strong influence on family members and all those touched by the family's various enterprises.

This paper describes the journey of long-term resilient families over three to more than six generations. These families pursue business opportunities together while passing their legacy values, culture and resources to each new generation. While few family enterprises reach this milestone, those that do amass impressive resources.

They are more than businesses; they also share a **family culture** of relationships, values, traditions, respect, and learning that underlies their business capabilities. Their family culture is the foundation of their business acumen. They dominate the economies of many countries because they are able to innovate and pursue opportunities with sustained commitment and resources. We call them **generative families** because of their vitality, creativity, and ability to continually reinvent themselves over generations.

Generative families are rare, unique, and important. In a time when the lifespan of businesses is declining, these enterprises represent a rare species that sustain consistent control over a long period of time. In fact, if a business is still operating over the course of two generations, it is very likely to be family-owned. These companies are important because, unlike so many business ventures that focus only on current profits, they endure long-term with values that transcend profitability. They stand for something, offering lessons that can be profitably learned not just by family business in their first generation but also by non-family enterprises that want to operate with values beyond the bottom line.

This is the fifth working paper[1] in an ongoing research project that opens the curtain on the private worlds of the most long-lasting and successful global family enterprises. We call them **generative** or **legacy families** to celebrate their resiliency and hardiness. They are **generative** because rather than depleting or consuming resources, they add to and amplify the various forms of family wealth. **A generative family uses its resources not just to sustain what they have but to create something new. The family extends its legacy—the family members' values and practices—in new directions that add not just to the family's financial wealth but also to its human, social, relationship, and spiritual "capital."** The ability to adapt, renew, and reinvent in response to challenge and adversity while sustaining a consistent culture and set of values is the essence of generativity. After creating success in a legacy business, each successive generation builds on this legacy, adding value through innovation, new ventures, and inspiring visions for family and business success.

---

1 The first working paper, **Three Pathways to Evolutionary Survival: Best Practices of Successful, Global, Multi-Generational Family Enterprises** (2012), presented survey data from 200 families. The second paper, **Good Fortune: Building a Hundred Year Family Enterprise** (2013), was an overview of the evolution of these families over generations. The third was **Releasing the Potential of the Rising Generation: How Long-Lasting Family Enterprises Prepare Their Successors** (2016), and the fourth was **Governing the Family Enterprise: The Evolution of Family Councils, Assemblies, and Constitutions** (2017).

HOW OPPORTUNISTIC INNOVATION, BUSINESS DISCIPLINE, AND A CULTURE OF STEWARDSHIP GUIDE THE JOURNEY ACROSS GENERATIONS

Given that so few families survive with both financial fortunes and family relationships intact, we wanted to learn how this wonderful achievement occurred, so more families can duplicate their success. While they began with a legacy business, we view them here as evolving **families**, not just businesses, sharing a changing portfolio of assets and business ventures.

By the third generation, most generative families shift from being a **family business**—one in which family needs and dynamics are primary—to becoming an **enterprising family** that stewards strong professional enterprises that run on clear, firm, and effective business principles. To accomplish this, the family has to step back from active management and adhere to a new sort of discipline. This disengagement may bring up certain difficulties: For example, how to deal with family members accustomed to perks and entitlements? How to maintain the values that the family stands for—the spirit of the family enterprise—as the business becomes more rational and professional? We discuss these questions below.

Our focus is on the extended family moving across generations. Along its journey, an enterprising family may own and control multiple enterprises, including:

- Privately held companies

- Public companies with the family remaining in control

- A holding company for multiple family enterprises and assets

- A family office to manage and coordinate family assets and activities

- Trusts that own assets for beneficiaries

- A family foundation for charitable and philanthropic endeavors

These types of enterprises often overlap. For example, a privately held family business might include a few non-family owners or investors. Stock in a public company may be held by a family trust or a family holding company. The family might own several business entities, each with their own boards but with family owners making the major decisions.

Each generation creates a new story and forges a new path. The story is not only about continuing what came before but opening a new chapter with new directions. Innovation and entrepreneurship does not begin and end with the initial wealth creator; instead, each generation takes different paths to reach new milestones. Each venture is the vehicle that provides a foundation for the next stage of family enterprise.

My bookshelf features more than 40 volumes with histories of families from our study. They feature inspiring origin stories: a founding patriarch, for example, who rises from humble roots and sees an opportunity, or the transformational products and services created by dedicated and passionate family members and employees. The books reproduce family pictures of stern couples and playful children and how each new generation contributed to the enterprise. Businesses get sold or expand globally, bringing the family's values and vision into an ever-wider playing field. No matter how disciplined and professional the business becomes, however, it still expresses the family's spirit and values in its business practices. Because we have promised our families anonymity we have not specified their location[2], type of business or other qualities that could identify them. But in this and previous working papers, we can present their stories in their own words.

---

2 Since a little more than half our families are from North America, we only specify when a family we quote is from another region.

RESILIENCE OF 100-YEAR FAMILY ENTERPRISES

THE 100-YEAR FAMILY RESEARCH PROJECT

Our research has been going on for nearly five years. We[3] have interviewed nearly 90 families across 20 countries. These extraordinarily successful families met three criteria:

Business/Financial Success. Created a successful business or set of businesses, with annual revenues of more than US$200M. 44% of our families have a net worth of over $1B. Still nearly 80% of our families continue to own their operating business.

Adaptability Over Generations. Successfully navigated at least two generational transitions with control being passed to the third (or later) generation.

Shared Family Identity. Retained a shared connection and identity with practices and processes that sustained values as an extended family.

Our intention was to gather personal accounts about what they did and how they did it. We interviewed a family leader from each family at length and in depth. (We interviewed two family members from different generations in about 20% of the families.) We asked them to describe their evolution over generations and tell stories that describe not just what they did but how they were able to do it. Among the families in our study are many renowned families from different countries, many of whom are household names.

This paper presents their direct words in stories that illustrate how they have thrived as loving, connected families. The stories also demonstrate what they did to produce new generations of committed, active innovators who added capability, complexity, and new directions to the expanding extended family.

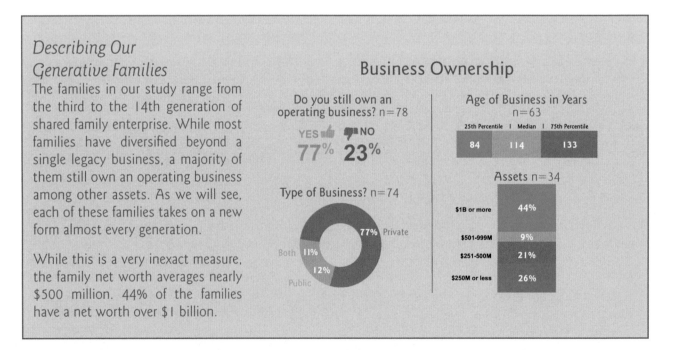

Describing Our Generative Families
The families in our study range from the third to the 14th generation of shared family enterprise. While most families have diversified beyond a single legacy business, a majority of them still own an operating business among other assets. As we will see, each of these families takes on a new form almost every generation.

While this is a very inexact measure, the family net worth averages nearly $500 million. 44% of the families have a net worth over $1 billion.

3 The research has been a team effort since its inception, with a group of highly experienced professionals conducting interviews. This team includes Peter Begalla, Emily Bouchard, Jane Flanagan, James Grubman, Charlotte Lamp, Isabelle Lescent-Giles, Susan Massenzio, Joshua Nacht, Michael O'Neal, Jamie Trager-Muney, and Keith Whitaker.

Our families represent every sector of the world:

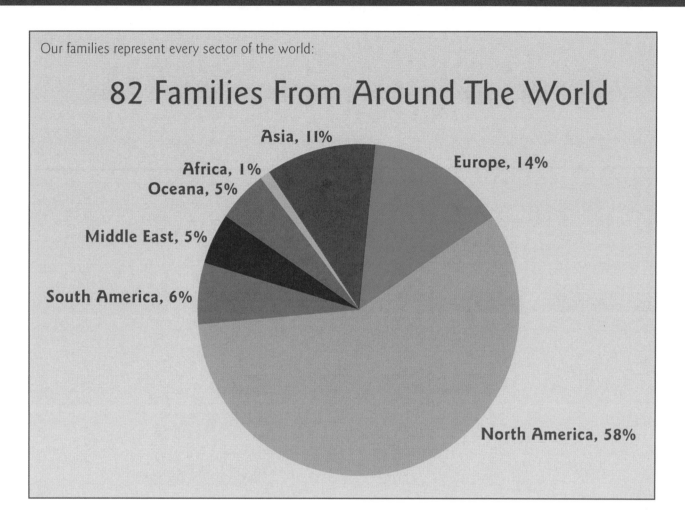

82 Families From Around The World

- Asia, 11%
- Europe, 14%
- Africa, 1%
- Oceana, 5%
- Middle East, 5%
- South America, 6%
- North America, 58%

RESILIENCE OF 100-YEAR FAMILY ENTERPRISES

The families have moved into and beyond the third generation of family leadership. There are large numbers of family members in each generation, and the number grows with each succeeding generation:

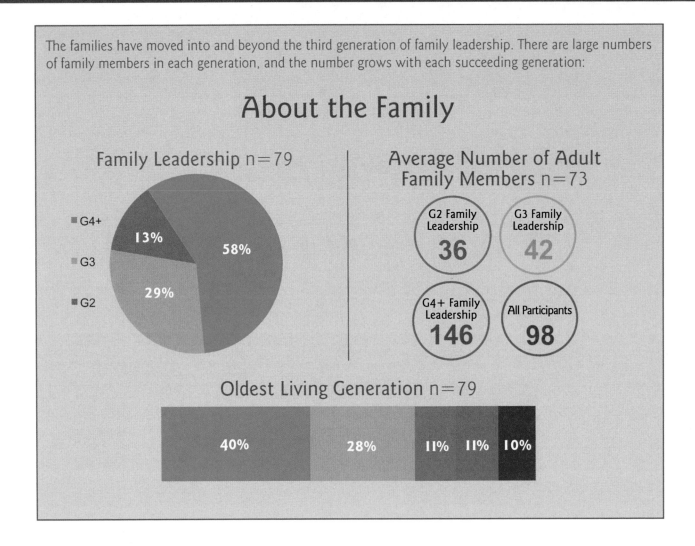

About the Family

Family Leadership n=79
- G4+ — 13%
- G3 — 58%
- G2 — 29%

Average Number of Adult Family Members n=73

G2 Family Leadership	G3 Family Leadership
36	42

G4+ Family Leadership	All Participants
146	98

Oldest Living Generation n=79

40% | 28% | 11% | 11% | 10%

HOW OPPORTUNISTIC INNOVATION, BUSINESS DISCIPLINE, AND A CULTURE OF STEWARDSHIP GUIDE THE JOURNEY ACROSS GENERATIONS

Overview of Paper

Generative families represent only a very small fraction of family businesses. The paper describes the features that characterize the "evolutionary pathways" of generative families. As their stories unfold, you will see how each family faces numerous challenges. Significant changes occur along with important market events. After each transition, the family redefines itself and moves forward in a new direction. Each new direction adds wealth to the family, as the family grows and adds various enterprises. We illuminate the nature of their resiliency and their ability to continually transform themselves while sustaining a consistent core of shared culture, values, and identity.

Part Two gives an overview of the patterns of adaption and renewal in these families: how they continually remake themselves. The **generative alliance** refers to three forces that unite to enable their spectacular success: the **legacy values and culture** of the family, **professional business discipline** together with structures that develop a strong and effective business, and **opportunistic innovation** that allows the family to continually seek new avenues for the family enterprise. This alliance of forces allows the family to continually reinvent itself as it crosses generations.

Then, in Part Three, we look at the four major transformations along the developmental path of most of our families:

● **Harvesting** of the legacy business to generate resources for further development;

● **Pruning** family ownership so that the owners are all aligned and committed to family enterprise development;

● **Diversifying** to develop a portfolio approach for their enterprises;

● **Grounding** to create a center and focus for the family, in most cases as a family office.

Part Four describes several consistent qualities that characterize the cultural similarities of generative families, qualities that encourage the flourishing of the generative alliance. We discovered that the older the family enterprise, the more pronounced were each of these qualities. These six cultural qualities, common across different countries, appear to differentiate generative families from business families that do not survive multiple generations:

● Long-term commitment

● Extension of family values to business

● Disciplined, focused, professional business

● Deepening the talent pool: Collaboration with non-family leadership

● Professionalization of family leaders

● Entrepreneurial attitude encouraged in each new generation

Part Five looks at how clear business governance, especially the formation of a board with independent members, focuses and aligns the business activity of these large, diverse, and multi-faceted families. We end with speculation about future prospects for generative families.

RESILIENCE OF 100-YEAR FAMILY ENTERPRISES

Overcoming Prevalent Myths about Family Business

One of our objectives is to challenge certain myths that have grown up about family business. Although the study of family enterprise only began in the mid-1980s, it has since become a sizable global activity in itself. Several common misconceptions limit their perspective. The actual experience of "generative" families—those that have succeeded both as businesses and as families beyond the third generation—challenges these myths.

Here are a few prevalent myths:

1. Family business faces a predestined decline across three generations.

As they repeat the observation "shirtsleeves to shirtsleeves" and observe data that few family businesses reach the third-generation, many business families have internalized a belief that business growth occurs only in the first generation. Then, the myth continues, there is decline or stagnation in the second generation if the business does not evolve into a traditionally managed business with minimal family involvement. The role of the third-generation cousins is simply to step back and allow professionals to run things. Our picture of generative families, however, is not a path of linear and front-loaded development followed by decline. Rather, generative families follow a cycle of continual change and reinvention across generations.

2. Wealth creation takes place largely through the achievement of a single entrepreneur in the first generation.

While the founders clearly make an incredible contribution, in many of our families they were only the first of a series of wealth creators. The founders often begin their enterprise with a sibling or cousin who they can trust and who shares their drive and vision. Several founders, for example, developed small unremarkable businesses that became super-charged with the addition of a son or daughter who lead expansion and growth. A generative family enterprise often has several different wealth creators, in successive generations.

3. Wealth creation mostly results from founding one successful business.

So goes the myth. But, in reality, business success includes several seminal activities. Initial success must be followed by additional, less newsworthy, activities to sustain the business. A good local manufacturing business may move across national borders or create new products under the leadership of second or third generation family leaders. War, social upheaval, or technological shifts might force a successful business to reinvent itself. A mature business produces capital to move into new areas, and each successive event spearheads further wealth creation.

4. Sale of the legacy business marks the end of the family enterprise.

While the sale of the legacy business is a huge transition for an extended family, generative families make an explicit commitment to renew the family and reorganize as a business family.

HOW OPPORTUNISTIC INNOVATION, BUSINESS DISCIPLINE, AND A CULTURE OF STEWARDSHIP GUIDE THE JOURNEY ACROSS GENERATIONS

5. Business success occurs because the family moves away from involvement and influence.[4]

The most demeaning myth about family business is that family businesses are "lesser" businesses that have to evolve into professional enterprises by removing the emotional bonds of the family. The reality of our generative families is that the business is built on a deep foundation of family culture and values about how to do business. This family culture sets values about trust, respect for employees and customers, a professional work ethic, long-term vision, and innovation. These qualities sustain the vitality of the business over generations. Professional businesses that lack these cultural values may have great difficulty sustaining innovation and growth, just as non-family businesses with similar values may tend to be more successful. The presence of the family as owners (even if they include non-family owners as well) is the generative engine for the business. While family values and practices can certainly undermine the business in some cases, generative families minimize the ways that the family drains the business while optimizing the positive qualities added by the family.

4 Our research builds upon the pioneering work of Danny Miller and Isabel La Breton-Miller whose book **Managing for the Long Run**, (Harvard Business School Press, 2005) pointed out the positive nature of the family culture in successful family enterprises.

RESILIENCE OF 100-YEAR FAMILY ENTERPRISES

Part Two – The Resilience of the Generative Family Enterprise: Continual Adaptation and Renewal

In the early years of the family business field, the family was viewed as inseparable from their legacy business. This view held that without the business, a family lost not just its livelihood but its identity. The experience of 100-year families, however, is quite different. They are not single businesses owned by a family so much as ever-changing business partnerships. These partnerships share a business legacy, values, and culture as they navigate through a turbulent environment. A single successful business may provide the initial thrust, but sustaining and growing family wealth demands skills exercised over many lifetimes. This is not an easy task as we can see from stories of family wealth squandered by heirs and successors. Passing on the dedication, creativity, vitality, and innovation of the founding generation across new generations is a challenge of the highest order. How that happens is more about the nature of the extended family as a family than about wealth creation by any particular business. A generative family goes through multiple reinventions.

There are certain common features in the **culture** and **mindset** of our generative families. The generative family has a drive to adapt, change, and innovate. Their unique evolution begins with the business and financial values of the founder—values that are then sustained and expressed by each successive generation. They are expressed in the policies and practices that enable the family to overcome emerging challenges and bring forth their unique vision. By explaining this developmental arc, we hope to inspire and educate other families on this path.

To succeed, a business family must build a resilient business culture able to anticipate and overcome crises as they emerge while becoming stronger in the process. Adaptation is a challenge for any business, but when a family is involved, the task is even more difficult. This is because families have a tendency to be conservative and uphold the status quo; the tradition of parental authority, for example, can limit their ability to change. By contrast, to our surprise, we found that the wisdom of the generative family enterprise lies in their resiliency in the face of change.

Generative families are growing **families** that have banded together to conduct business. Their legacy business is the initial vehicle for family livelihood but not the only one. Over several generations, generative families move from a single successful venture to multiple business entities that continually seek opportunities to diversify in new directions. But they achieve this while also remaining a close, connected, and consistent family, sharing and teaching values and skills to each new generation that moves into leadership.

Challenges Within and Without

During the 100-year journey, continual change and evolution is necessary because the family faces emerging challenges from inside and outside:

- **Within the family,** each new generation brings more people and a different range of talents and desires. Older generations die off and new family members must organize, make decisions, and align their different skills, values, and visions.

- **Outside, the business environment** is unforgiving, with disasters and new directions beckoning. Each generation has to steer their business and financial entities across different terrain.

Today, such changes occur more rapidly in our globally connected world. One seventh generation family leader observed that for six generations, things were predictable and orderly. The business passed from first son to first son, with the business operating in the same way with skilled craftsmen and laborers. During the past 20 years, however, they experienced more change than all previous generations combined. The business environment became global, technology was transformed, and competition emerged from everywhere. Internally, the family decided that all family members—sons and daughters, younger and older—were eligible for leadership positions.

Families strongly resist change. Many business founders and leaders want things to simply continue as they have because they have known nothing but success. Many business families fail because they are unable to retain the spark of creativity that could create value for the new generation. In these cases, businesses may become stale and vulnerable. Conflict may erupt, calling the direction and leadership into question. Family members worry how they can avoid decline.

As business founders age, they tend to harvest their success and grow weary of having to reinvent themselves. Indeed, a core aspect of the ability to change is skill in deciding when to "harvest" the value of a family asset by its sale. This sale can free the family to pursue new opportunities as new generations, with different perspectives, emerge.

CONTINUAL REINVENTION

What does it take to sustain continual business innovation and adaptation? Resilient businesses approach a turbulent environment by anticipating and adapting rather than reacting. There are some general patterns and principles by which they navigate change.

A common model for the growth and development of a business is the S-curve. A founder with limited resources struggles to build a successful business, and the business then succeeds in a spurt of exponential growth. But growth cannot continue forever. The curve eventually levels off or declines as products mature, competition emerges, or technology and tastes change. The business now faces a crisis and must find a new pathway to growth or face decline. A family enterprise may experience periods of exponential growth, but its continued success rides on the family's ability to renew themselves when growth slows or crisis strikes.

Generative families seek opportunities to create new S-curves or extend current ones. They jump from a maturing or declining effort into the development of new products or markets or a new venture or investment. When they undertake a deep transformation in their business, they begin a new S-curve:

They buy and sell, innovate, and renew while continually redesigning and shifting their business activity. They can do this as Craftsmen by innovating their core product or technology, or as Opportunists by seeking out new business ventures.

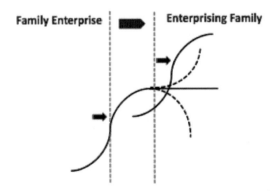

RESILIENCE OF 100-YEAR FAMILY ENTERPRISES

Few generations begin and end with the same business in the same place. The enterprise might face **external** threats like the pervasiveness of social media, global competition for core products, new global brands, the aftermath of war and political threats, or maturing and obsolete products. Enterprises can't wait too long; they have to anticipate and respond to challenges. If the family's only asset is a single business, the threat is especially severe. The old leaders are mortal; they must find innovators within the family who have the will and the skill not just to sustain their vision but to adapt and change.

Our research allows us to see the journey over three or more generations of each generative family. By asking each family about the key events in their family and business evolution, we can see that every family is on a multi-generational journey, filled with emerging challenges, opportunities and large and small changes in the family and business. For each family we can create a time line outlining the twists and turns over time. While, as we will see, many of the changes and transformations have similar patterns, a version of the graphic below can be developed for each family to show the sequence and nature of the key events in their history. In fact, several of our families have drawn their own family journey map:

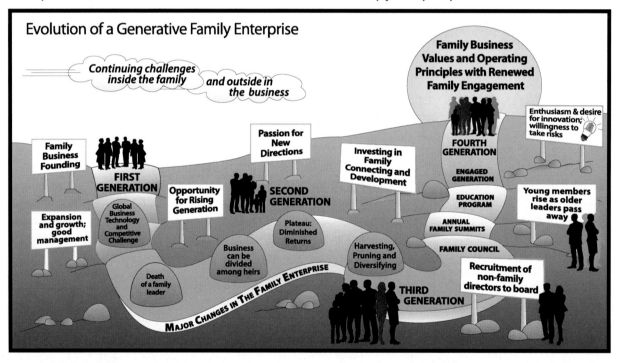

Innovation and entrepreneurship are not the sole province of the founding generation. Generative families develop family talent that enables them to redefine themselves in each new generation. They experience a continual tension between maintaining the status quo, "harvesting" wealth, and investing in innovation for the long term. The family has to deal with dissent and agree on a direction; generative families accomplish this successfully. By their fourth generation, few remain in the business they began generations earlier.

The change capability of generative families is often due to the initiative of their "rising" generation. The young successors are not satisfied with accepting the status quo as lucrative as that may be. They are anxious to prove themselves and excited about new directions. Their global education has taught them new ideas and possibilities, but to put their skills and knowledge to the service of the family, they need support from their elders. The rising generation needs to listen and learn from the elders' wisdom and experience before charging off in a new direction.

HOW OPPORTUNISTIC INNOVATION, BUSINESS DISCIPLINE, AND A CULTURE OF STEWARDSHIP GUIDE THE JOURNEY ACROSS GENERATIONS

Surviving a Crisis

After a generation or more of success, businesses may face a crisis: new technology, business recessions, increasing competition, or the need for reinvestment capital can challenge the business. Here are two examples:

Family 1. After surviving a world war and occupation, one of our families found themselves in a country where they were not welcome. Three third generation cousins pooled their considerable skills in international trade, and each of them moved to a different country. They ended up creating three new businesses, all of which grew and thrived far beyond the scope of their original business.

Family 2. After three generations of success with an iconic product, another family business saw that new technology was making their product obsolete. But the company had tremendous recognition and affection. A third-generation family leader after business school and apprenticeship at a consulting firm, was asked to come aboard and redefine the business. After exploring people's perceptions of the company and its products, the family came up with a new mission that led them in new directions but with a continued focus on consumer goods. Their reputation gave them visibility, while the new leader moved manufacturing offshore and created a new generation of products. He helped employees who were displaced by the transition to find new jobs and rebuild their obsolete factory as a product development center. The company successfully leveraged its legacy of brand recognition to a new generation of customers and products.

Craftsmen and Opportunists: Two Business Success Strategies

Families may pursue two broad strategies of business development across generations: First, the drive to perfection of the **Craftsman** who builds a product or competency better than anyone else, one that enables it to defend and thrive within a niche. Second, the initiative of the **Opportunist,** whose curiosity, adaptability, intelligence, and willingness to risk leads to success in many diverse areas.

● **CRAFTSMAN:** The Craftsman develops the special capability of **doing something better than anyone else.** They extend and develop a single S-curve. Many of our families created a product or a technology that served a need, and they competed with larger entities by producing great products and being exceptionally responsive to customers. They created a disciplined, productive, cost efficient, professional business. And, as they kept creating better products, they moved to supply larger and larger markets. Whether these products were industrial supplies, books, shipping, consumer goods, or food products, they often created strong brands that became global or focused on a technology that was hard to duplicate. Companies like these become market leaders in specialized areas that other companies find it hard to enter. They often create the technology early, continually reinvest in new products, and expand into new markets with their core capability. This path is exemplified by the German Mittelstand[5] companies that succeed with patient and focused effort, develop brands known for quality, and build effective and disciplined businesses.

● **OPPORTUNIST:** Opportunists adapt by **seeking out and seizing upon new opportunities.** Like traders, they are always looking for good deals. They take the family onto a new S-curve, developing diversity by cultivating different strengths in family and non-family leaders. For instance, one family in the cattle business while on their annual drive to market in the cities, noticed that certain spots were

5 Simon, Hermann. **Hidden Champions of the 21st Century**. Springer, 2009. He defines a group of mostly privately-held, high growth companies that are skilled and focused on a clearly defined area. 2/3 of them are family controlled, a detail that he does not focus on but notes that of this group, half of them have moved into a phase of non-family leadership. His findings mirror what we found.

becoming centers for grazing and commerce. They bought land and acquired companies in these areas. Families like this one develop a portfolio of assets and are not sentimental about selling those assets that no longer produce. They are entrepreneurial and continually pursue innovation and new ideas.

While either of these styles is effective on its own, many of our generative families have adopted both of these styles, pursuing them at different stages of their evolution. These families develop effective professional businesses that are also opportunistic in seeking and moving in new directions. Sometimes different generations or unusual situations require a focus on one style or the other, but the alternative style remains important as well. The two styles represent different capabilities exhibited by the family at different times. Generative families are not undermined by conflict between the craftsman and opportunist styles but appreciate that there is a time and a place for each one and that they must co-exist. At different times one or the other may be in ascendance.

THE GENERATIVE STAKEHOLDER ALLIANCE

Generative families move forward at different times along the divergent developmental paths of craftsmen and opportunists. Creating a single, aligned, disciplined, innovative business that is adaptive and vital in a changing global business environment is a wonderful achievement. But it is not enough! A disciplined business can easily become stale and lose its vitality to a competitor or new technology or simply lose its drive or focus. To counter this tendency, a family enterprise must also remain entrepreneurial, opportunistic, and open to discovering new paths with new ventures. This requires a different mindset and skills, as the enterprise rediscovers some features of the higher risk, more improvisational style of the business founder.

Generative families have the capacity to act as both craftsmen and opportunists by drawing on the talent and energy of different stakeholders. Business leaders recruited from outside the family are joined by entrepreneurial, innovative members of new rising family generations. Generative family enterprises exhibit a unique ability to blend these two kinds of energy—energies that are not usually present in non-family ventures. They are able to do this because they also have consistent values and culture. We call this combination of business discipline, entrepreneurial expansiveness, and legacy culture and values the **Generative Stakeholder Alliance.** The emergence of this alliance is a key element in achieving success across multiple generations.

The first element of this alliance is **Legacy,** the contribution of the founders. In the process of developing a successful and fast-growing business, they articulate and maintain a **foundation of legacy values, policies, and practices** that they share with family members in the next generation. This foundation forms an enduring organizational culture that family and non-family members can depend upon. The knowledge that the family is committed to these principles over the long-term creates a safe and comfortable environment for collaboration and trust. This commitment creates a culture where family members, employees, and the outside community all know what the business and the family stand for.

Building upon this foundation of values and culture, the family develops a strong business that continues to do something really well; the **Craftsmen** path. After their initial success, the family invests in building a business structure, culture, and discipline that will enable the further development of the enterprise. It continues to create new products and expand into different markets. It moves from an improvisational founder-oriented style of operation to one where capable and talented people with business skills are in charge. These managers include non-family members who will support and augment the talents of family leaders.

We saw a common pattern in the second or third generation, as Craftsmanship leads to a more disciplined, professional business. Many rising generation family members take on redefined roles as owners who do not directly manage business operations. The family partners with non-family leaders who share their values and vision and add new skills the family does not have. We also see a shift from a single legacy business to owning a portfolio of ventures. Family members no longer expect to be business operators; they are now **owners** looking to add to and sustain family wealth.

But a family enterprise cannot succeed long-term simply as a good craftsman with a single business. New challenges emerge, and the family enterprise must develop and transform itself in major ways. They have to be open to finding new directions and employing the talents and interests of new family members who are growing to maturity. In addition to being craftsmen, they also have to become, or remain, **Opportunists.** This is the third element in the generative stakeholder alliance.

The Generative Alliance

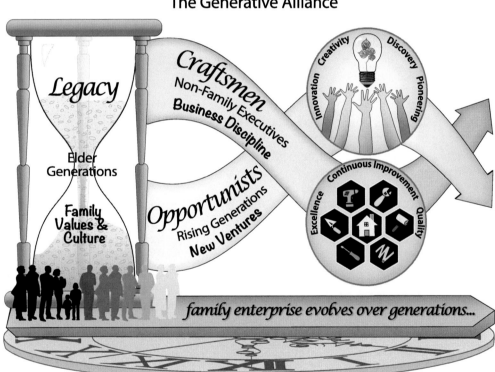

family enterprise evolves over generations...

Stakeholders of the Generative Alliance

Three contributing groups of stakeholders blend their skills and perspectives to create this alliance:

- **Elders** from the founding generations who pass on their deep lifetime commitment to family values to the business and their family heirs.

- **Professional leaders** and executives who share the family values and who contribute their expertise gained from their experience in other businesses.

- **Rising generation** family members who, through their education and outside experience, value innovation and challenge the other two groups to take risks and find new opportunities.

RESILIENCE OF 100-YEAR FAMILY ENTERPRISES

	CORE VALUES	DEFINITION	STAKEHOLDERS
LEGACY *Foundational Culture*	**Tradition** Trust, Fairness, Respect, Stewardship, Integrity	Enduring business values, policies and traditions of prior generations	Elders, founding generation
CRAFTSMEN *Business Discipline*	**Excellence** Quality, Continuous Improvement	Creating a great business by doing something better than everybody else	Family business operators, non-family executives
OPPORTUNISTS *Entrepreneurship*	**Innovation** Creativity, Discovery, Pioneering	Anticipating change and seeking new, innovative opportunities	New generation family members, with education and experience in new areas

In a generative family, these three elements work in harmony. Each stakeholder group respects the roles and focus of the others. Elders, non-family leaders, and rising generation each work in their own areas. Because they form a shared family enterprise, they interact in a non-hierarchical way; each group has a voice and no group has precedence over the others. Through governance and collaboration, they develop the integration, coordination, and resource sharing that blends the capabilities of each stakeholder group.

Still, there is frequently **creative tension** among the stakeholder groups for resources and attention. While many families emphasize one orientation over the others during one period, generative families find the wisdom to value all three elements and make choices that support them working together. While one group or the other may take precedence at different times, the generative family seems able to adopt a mindset and policies that manage and balance these differences.

The remainder of this paper offers many examples of how the unique opportunity and balance of this generative stakeholder alliance creates vital, enduring family enterprises.

HOW OPPORTUNISTIC INNOVATION, BUSINESS DISCIPLINE, AND A CULTURE OF STEWARDSHIP GUIDE THE JOURNEY ACROSS GENERATIONS

STORY #1: CROSSROADS COMMERCE: THE DEVELOPMENT ARC OF A REPRESENTATIVE GENERATIVE FAMILY

This 100-year, six generation family contains periods of fast growth, plateaus, and innovation and change. Each one ushered in major changes in the enterprises, or how the family realigned to include a new generation. Change can be anticipated, and changes set in motion, or change emerge out of a crisis such as death of a family leader or unexpected business crisis. The story of Crossroads Commerce (a pseudonym) illustrates how the Generative Alliance anticipates, initiates change, and sustains family resiliency at each generational and business transition point.

Crossroads Commerce was founded in 1880. The founder moved to a newly thriving farming community. Seeing opportunity, he bought a general store and began to buy farmland with federal homestead assistance. His brother and sister moved to the community and joined him, and both the farm and the store prospered. The founding brother had two sons and a daughter who also entered the business.

Tragedy struck when the founder died in an accident while still in his prime. His oldest son took over and ran the business ably. His brother helped on the farm and his sister helped out in the store. Ownership passed equally to the three first generation siblings, and they formed three family ownership branches. They bought more farmland and stores in other communities, and both the stores and the farms benefitted from their good management.

By the third generation, the dozen family owners divided into two divisions: farming and a commercial division. The sister's children moved to another city and sold some of their shares to the remaining branches. The businesses prospered but stayed on a long plateau with little innovation. There were early cross-generation transitions. The three sons who ran the businesses passed away at early ages, pushing young members of the third generation into leadership roles. After a year of marriage, when his father-in-law died suddenly, a young lawyer who married a third-generation daughter was asked to join the board of directors. His mother-in-law was overwhelmed by the demands of being on the board of directors and saw him as a promising resource. He eventually became CEO and chair of the board; at that time, the board consisted of two family members from each branch. He was trusted by all and was able to mediate between the interests and personalities of the three branches.

These young third generation family leaders began to innovate and change. After many years, they were seeing diminished returns at a time when they had to meet the needs of more than 50 family members. The family had many loyal employees who respected their stewardship, but family members no longer worked in the business. The board, however, was active and hands-on. Family board members "ran" each division—farms and retail. Their business faced no competition for many years, but now they needed innovation and renewal in both businesses.

They entered a new rapid-growth phase. The family recruited experienced non-family independent directors to the board. These independent directors added further expertise to the non-family managers on the farms and in the stores. The fourth generation of the family initiated a flurry of innovations in the business. They recruited two more directors with experience in new technology for farming and retailing. The independent directors helped them develop a growth plan, as the fourth generation expressed a desire to take greater risks. Their aim was to expand both businesses, especially the commercial division which had the capacity to grow rapidly.

The fourth generation's enthusiasm and desire for innovation challenged the complacency of their parents, who, nonetheless, allowed them the opportunity to put their ideas to work. However, many members of generation four had grown up detached from the business and did not feel connected or informed. So, with the support of the aging third generation, the family affirmed their core values as they educated and reached out to their children.

RESILIENCE OF 100-YEAR FAMILY ENTERPRISES

As they focused on recruiting outside talent for the board and in management, the family also began an active process of engaging the emerging fourth generation. They created a family council as the board became more professional and independent, and the focus of learning and innovative energy shifted to this council. The council began holding family summits each year and began an active educational program to teach business and financial literacy skills to young family owners. The result was that the fourth generation became not just interested but also engaged and informed about the business.

The council actively supported the board in investing in new ideas and developing a plan for growth and innovation. They also perceived that the two businesses were very interdependent and feared that a downturn could hurt both businesses at once. So they initiated a search to acquire a new operating business that would diversify the family. At the same time, they sold some of their farmland to generate capital for an acquisition. Presently, the fourth generation has taken over the family board positions in addition to leadership on the family council, and the fifth generation is benefitting from the renewed family engagement developed by their parents.

Looking over the development of this family enterprise over four generations, we can see each element of the generative alliance. First, there was business development followed by innovation guided by a core of family values that emphasized a long-term commitment to excellence. In order to make all these elements work together, each generation developed a more complex and increasingly professional system of governance that fostered both family connection and business excellence.

THE STRUCTURE OF RESILIENCE

Generative families are characterized by **how** they handle planned and unplanned transitions—the degree to which they anticipate and respond to emerging challenges. Behind their success, there is often a struggle inside the family, first about whether to change and then about how to accomplish it. After each transition, they develop increasingly complex business and governance structures to manage their growing enterprises and family.

Family enterprises, even generative ones, make mistakes. One new family leader initiated the purchase of a competitor, telling the family he would make it work. It didn't. As a result, the family learned to be more involved in such decisions. Another enterprise was not performing well when the new generation took over. They didn't want to sell, so instead, they cut costs and reduced family perks in order to turn the business around. After this wrenching change, they had to rebuild family relationships. The overreaction was forgivable; in fact, their continued success stems from their willingness to forgive and move on.

Every family gets stuck or faces crises. Those that do not survive are done in by them. Generative families, on the other hand, are not just lucky--they develop the readiness and skill to rebound. They do not experience change is unexpected or unwanted; instead, they find ways to anticipate and respond that leave them in better shape than before. In the coming sections, we'll look at the common transformations these families make to adapt to continual change as well as the cultural consistencies and governance mechanisms that allow them to be so resilient.

All businesses and families face continual changes and crises. Unanticipated changes, like the early death of a key family leader or the emergence of new technologies can tear a business apart. Generative families, however, act decisively in response to each challenge. At best, the family anticipates a crisis or at least sees an early warning sign.

HOW OPPORTUNISTIC INNOVATION, BUSINESS DISCIPLINE, AND A CULTURE OF STEWARDSHIP GUIDE THE JOURNEY ACROSS GENERATIONS

We see a three-phase resilience cycle in how generative families respond to change:

- **Prepare/Anticipate:** Even when they are not preparing for a specific change, the family expects and anticipates broad general changes such as the need to develop a new generation of family members or prepare for a shift of customers or products. They notice early warning signs and face their import.

- **Engage/Decide:** As a change approaches, the family gathers to consider what it means. They engage multiple family members and listen to differing points of view before they take action.

- **Redefine/Renew:** After the change, the family does not go back to the way things were. They find a new path and work to implement it. While they respect tradition, they are able to let go of anything that is obsolete.

It's not simply the presence of change but this cycle of adaption and resilience that differentiates the generative family.

Cycle of Adaptation and Resilience

Another way of viewing resiliency is as a **learning mindset.** Rather than trying to dominate and impose their will, family leaders are open to new ideas from inside and outside the family. Businesses that exhibit resilience in the face of continual change have been characterized as **learning organizations.** The quality to question old ways and experiment with new ones is an aspect of resiliency, especially important to counteract the conservative tendency of the family owners. Without learning there cannot be real change.

Dealing with Pitfalls

In spite of their best efforts, however, there are many pitfalls that can derail a family enterprise. They can over-expand or become too focused on family politics while neglecting the external challenges. A business family might think too highly of themselves and over-value their business. They may idealize their values to the extent that they ignore signs that they are not living up to them. In order to bring such tendencies to the surface, one family decided that *"…we should have an advisor as an ombudsman for family members who don't feel comfortable coming directly to another family member with a complaint or suggestion. We depend on her for content at the family meetings."*

RESILIENCE OF 100-YEAR FAMILY ENTERPRISES

By facing challenges or issues that may be buried or ignored, the family becomes aware of the impending need for change. The initiative for a major transformation often arises when a new generation comes into power. When a rising generation takes control, it's important that they take stock of what they have inherited and consider what is needed to sustain it. As one family member put it, *"The third generation received the reins of the business about 10-12 years ago, though, at that time, they were no longer young. One of their bravest decisions was to remove themselves from operations. Everyone that worked in the business left their executive positions, and they created new regulations among themselves to allow new leadership to emerge."*

Because generative families pay attention to warning signs, they quickly become aware of upcoming difficulties and latent signs of discord. According to one family member, *"It's easy when the company is doing well, but it all changes in a difficult business climate. You need to build shareholder relationships to prepare for tougher business times—for unforeseen economic or global transitions."* Another younger family member noted, *"We looked at our whole organization all the way down and made changes to fit our generation. We realized that our dynamic and needs were completely different from the older generation. The structures we had in place were obsolete. We worked for a year reevaluating our whole structure."*

Generative families are clear that the purpose of family enterprise is about values as much as profit. Poor business results can be a sign that the culture has not been attended to—or sometimes, good business results can divert attention from a company's culture and values. In the excerpt below, a third-generation leader tells of losing his way and the measures taken by the leaders to regain the company's values:

> *Another transition led us towards value-based leadership. From the early 90's to the 2000's, the company tripled in sales and increased approximately by a factor of nine. However, we lost our way relative to values, and I lost my way as the leader. I was terribly focused on acquisitions and new products growth, but I lost the how, the cultural part. We began focusing on the executive chain, working eight days a year on leadership development and value clarity. When we rolled this out to the company, employees started taking this stuff on and asking for more. We began to embody value-based leadership; in fact, these systems and processes are in place today. That was a single pivot point around culture in the history of the company.*

Family conflicts about business issues can be difficult for a family to resolve, but generative families are characterized by making tough decisions and carrying them out. Here's how one family handled conflict:

> *It's hard to work with your family members. Specifically, my father and one of his brothers have had a lot of differences; they hardly ever agree. One is extremely conservative and the other is more progressive, and this has caused a lot of issues over the years. For example, they argue a lot during the Board of Directors meeting. When the consultant came in he said, "My goodness, this needs to be settled. You have to resolve your differences." He had some strong conversations with them and tried to teach them conflict resolution skills. It helped but they still have their ups and downs.*

Summary

The first and second generation of a generative family builds a foundation of culture and values that leads them to be adaptive and resilient. As families and as businesses, they are open and transparent and able to learn and grow in their interactions. They fight the tendency to avoid or deny the need to change. They listen to the new voices of each generation, seek new ways of doing business, and learn from external resources and teachers. Their resiliency leads them on a continuing path that is punctuated by some major transformations, as we will see in the next section. It also enables them to develop capabilities that are reflected in their family business culture and in their governance mechanisms.

Taking Action In Your Own Family Enterprise

At the end of each section, we will suggest some ways of applying the insights we discussed to a family that is in an early stage of the journey toward becoming a generative family. You can do these activities on your own or together with members of your family as a shared learning activity. It's always better to do them together with other family members, especially with members of other generations.

In this section, we presented a view of the family enterprise as an evolving social system that must develop the capability to be open to continual change. As you look at your family across generations, here are some activities that you can do to reflect upon your own resiliency and change-ability.

Family Enterprise Timeline

As you learn about and explore the history of your family enterprise, you can see it as a journey that you can record on a timeline. This will be used to develop your family enterprise history. At the bottom of the paper, you should make a dateline showing the years. You can begin on the left with the date of the founding of the legacy enterprise (or another meaningful date such as the birthdate of the founder). Divide up the length of the paper with the years.

Next, fill in the date of the founding of the legacy business on the left, and about 4/5 of the way to the right side, make a line that is designated **Now.** Beyond this line, you can speculate and anticipate events that may happen in the future.

Now, begin to fill in the key events for the business and the family. You might divide the paper vertically into a top and bottom half. The top might portray business events and the bottom events related to the family. Some families construct a timeline together by placing a large sheet of butcher paper, several feet long, on the wall. You can then fill in dates and events using marker pens. Other methods include large post-it notes that can be moved around and family pictures related to major events. Whatever method you choose, in the end you will have a timeline of the key positive and negative events in your family and business history.

If you are building this timeline with other family members, start with the memories of the elders and then the recollections of the younger generations. Also, ask different people to recall the same event because people are likely to remember important events differently.

RESILIENCE OF 100-YEAR FAMILY ENTERPRISES

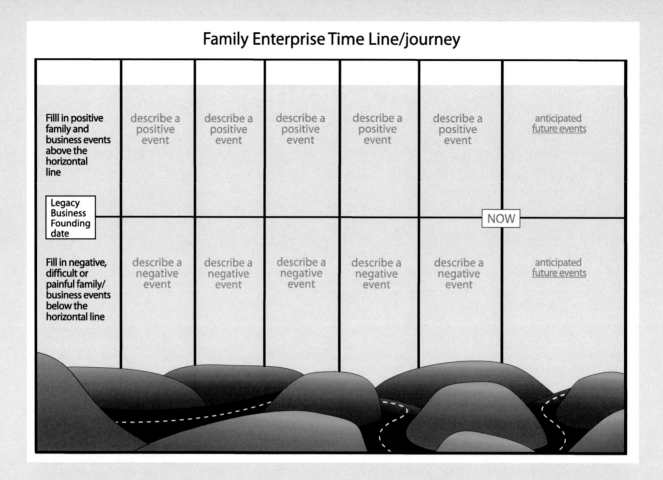

Resiliency

You, your family, and its various business enterprises have experienced many changes and turning points. Now, with the help of the timeline you constructed, consider how well you anticipated or responded to unexpected events as well as those that caused by your own actions. You can focus on each important positive and negative event, their consequences, and their impact.

As you reflect on each event, discuss what you did to prepare for or anticipate it. Then consider what was done afterwards to build on the new situation and take the family and family enterprise forward. You can talk about each of the three phases of change that were described: Preparing/Anticipating, Engaging/Deciding, and Redefining/Renewing. How did you family experience each stage? After you have looked at what was actually done, you might discuss how you could have approached and recovered from that event more effectively.

Generative Alliance

We have suggested that the essence of resilience as a family enterprise comes from your ability to listen to, respect, and combine the three elements of the Generative Alliance. As you look at your timeline and your response to change, consider how your family activates each element of the alliance:

- **Legacy**
  How does the family express and support its legacy values in its activities?

- **Craftsmanship**
  How does the family enterprise support and maintain excellence while offering better products and services than anyone else? What groups are at the center of this focus and effort?

- **Opportunism**
  How does the family find and exploit opportunities, try new things, and move in new directions? What groups are at the center of this focus and effort?

Future Casting

- Look ahead to the future and the changes you can prepare for and anticipate.

- Select a time in the short or medium future that makes sense to you such as the next 5 years—or a longer period like 10 or 20 years. Alternately, you might select an important date, such as the time a trust ends or when a family member plans to retire.

- Mark that event and imagine together what it will look like if you prepare for and respond to that change in a resilient, positive, successful manner. Generate a picture of what success will look like.

- Next, consider the most effective things that you as a family can do to prepare for and anticipate that event.

- Finally, consider what specific steps you and your family can take right now to begin to prepare for that event.

RESILIENCE OF 100-YEAR FAMILY ENTERPRISES

Part Three – Turning Points: Major Transformations of Generative Families

Family enterprises undergo huge transitions while crossing generations. They often sell their legacy business and restructure to become a family office with a portfolio of assets. As a family, they transition from a blood family to a "pruned" family united by choice, including only family members who actively choose to be part of this multi-generational business entity. Generative families are not only aware of necessary changes, they redesign and renew themselves after each one to emerge stronger and better. This section looks at how these major transformations influence both business and the family and propel them forward.

A majority of our generative families move along a path punctuated by four huge milestone transformations:

- **Harvesting** the legacy business and becoming an investing family;

- **Pruning** the family tree by buying out some family members, leaving only those committed to business ownership;

- **Diversifying** by buying other businesses and making other investments, thus creating a business portfolio;

- **Grounding** by creating a family office to centralize and oversee the multiple business entities and operations.

Each transformation deeply changes the nature of the family. The generative family emerges from each of these major transformations with a new focus that continues their legacy values and builds upon family strengths. They work actively through the resilience cycle to anticipate, redefine themselves, and work through changes. While families do not go through these milestones in strict order, the progression from single-family business with a few owners to a portfolio of enterprises with a family office and a pruned (but still sizeable) set of family owners defines the path of most of our generative families.

Evolution of the Family Enterprise

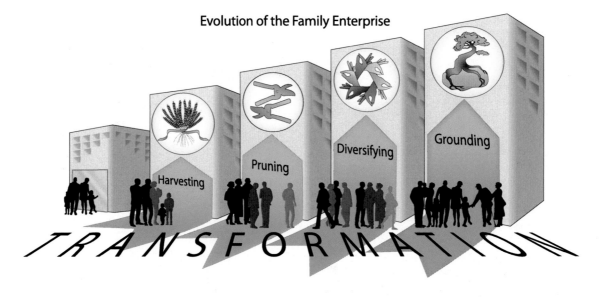

26

"HARVESTING" THE LEGACY BUSINESS[6]

When a wealth creator tells future generations, "Never sell the family business," the heirs are wise to take this admonition with a grain of salt. No business can last forever. A business-owning family does not wait for their business to fail. They look ahead and periodically ask:

- Does this business make sense for us now?

- Can we remain competitive and maintain our success in the face of new technology, globalization and social change?

- Can we handle and operate it as it should be managed?

- Do we have the resources to invest in sustaining excellence?

Each family in our study had a long-term view of their business and a deep personal commitment to their legacy. Most families wanted to hold onto their legacy businesses. But sometimes, even a strong and vibrant business can be threatened by external factors like social changes or new technology. One family, reluctantly and with great reservations, decided to sell their legacy business. A senior member of the family related:

> Nobody wanted to sell the company, but because we were offered a premium that was 67% higher than the day before, we felt we had to take the offer. We realized that if we turned down the offer, we'd have to allocate significant resources to rebuild the company, and this would involve major changes in leadership. We weren't sure whether we could persevere through the turmoil this would cause, so we ultimately decided to sell.

Some studies suggest that the sale of the legacy business means the end of the family as an organized entity. In our study, however, this is far from the case. The sale of the legacy business is a major transformation—a watershed event—but it leads generative families to a new beginning. Selling a business means transferring value for money and leaving the business behind. The term "harvest" refers to a family's departure from majority ownership of their legacy business because, for the family, the event is not an end. In agriculture, a harvest allows the field to regenerate and then be replanted. A family that harvests decides to take resources from a single business to nurture and develop other opportunities. The sale of assets can occur more than once; a few families report that they harvest a major asset every generation to offer some family members the chance to go on their own and other the opportunity to take on new challenges.

Half the families in our study "harvested" their legacy business. This has two transformative effects on the family:

- It allows some family members to cash out and leave the family partnership. Other family members choose to support their lives and individual family needs by remaining in the family partnership. Selling an asset is like letting pressure out of a pump; it allows the family to continue to operate while reducing pressure for continual returns on their invested assets.

- It allows the new generation to develop new businesses that employ their skills and meet the family's need for new sources of wealth. Several families had more than one major family business. By selling one of their assets that either needed new capital or was bringing slower and less predictable returns, they were able to refocus on new efforts and investments.

6 The harvest concept comes from Jay Hughes.

RESILIENCE OF 100-YEAR FAMILY ENTERPRISES

As a result of the harvest, our families commonly develop several sources of wealth--a holding company, family office or, perhaps, a private trust company that combines the benefits of a family office with that of a trust. Any of these arrangements enable them to buy and sell investments.

Even though the family may value its legacy business highly, there may be good reasons to pursue a harvest. While the business performed well in the past, it may be maturing, producing lower returns, or needing a significant infusion of capital. The enterprise may have grown to enormous proportions but attracted few family members to manage it. In cases like these, a family often feels comfortable detaching their identity from the business. Even though there may be sentimental ties to the business and its rich history, the family may decide to move on.

Who Decides?

Who makes this decision and how is it made? In most family businesses, the decision is made by only a few family members at the ownership or board level. They may not share an offer more broadly within the family because of confidentiality—or they may not feel the need to inform the family at all. We see a different process of decision making in generative families. Board members or key shareholders might make informed decisions, but they understand that due to the emotional significance of the proposed sale and the values of the family, non-owning family members should be consulted too. The younger generation, who stand to become owners in the future, are especially important to the family. Do they understand and agree with the values and challenges that are being considered in the sale? The generative family finds a way to engage the whole family in the conversation about the possible sale and solicits opinions before taking action.

Deciding to Hold On

Sometimes, upon listening to the voices of its members, a family may decide against a sale. Instead, they recommit the family's energy and resources to renewing the business. Here are three examples as related by members of each family:

> *Family 1. The challenge at this point was to bring in a non-family CEO. But we questioned whether he or she would be able to maintain the culture and the values that we have established. We have a very strong culture that is part of the fabric of our company. Part of our sadness about selling the business came from the feeling that we might lose this wonderful legacy and culture we've developed.*

> *Family 2: There has always been a strong commitment to the long-term ownership of the business. We've been approached countless times, even monthly, by venture capitalists or competitors who want to buy the business, but we've never even discussed these offers at the board level, because the family has made our policy clear. We simply say, "We're not interested," and move along. We have a commitment to maintaining the business for future generations.*

> *Family 3: If all the assets of the business were liquidated, everyone would have a bunch of money in their pockets. But we would just feel sick, like we let down our ancestors who built the business and never thought of selling it.*

Deciding to Sell

Despite the central role of the legacy business in sustaining family connection and identity, there may be business reasons to consider a sale. Here are a few examples of these situations:

> By the time the question came up about whether to sell the business, the family members were pretty distanced from the business. Most of them have professions, so the business is always in the background. That really represented the culture of the family when we decided to sell. That decision was actually initiated by non-family, non-executive directors who said, "You've had an amazing 90-year run, but now you're running a lot of risk. We're worried about the risk you're carrying as a family."

If they are not committed to the business, minority family owners can force a sale.

> They had an empire—all the land around the city center. But ultimately, they had to sell because the small shareholders wanted to sell. Often the small shareholders are unhappy and turn sour. And when someone turns sour, they start to act badly.

If the family does not have the will, skills, or resources to address emerging business needs, they can preempt a later crisis by a strategic choice to sell and diversify. For example, one family controlled a large but poorly performing public company. Content with their considerable dividends, they did not demand change until the downturn in performance worsened and threatened the dividend. The family was approached by a buyer who wanted to take the company in a different direction than the family wanted. Nevertheless, given the decline that had not been addressed, they felt they had to sell. As a public company, the deal was much in the news, and this made the very private family uncomfortable. They were glad to descend back under the radar after the sale was consummated.

It's important to note that family advisors may become a separate interest group of their own, and their own self-interest may further complicate, or even undermine, the situation. This family eventually sold because they lost connection and trust in the business:

> We had limited input to a trustee office that organized things for us. We should have learned 20 years before that we needed a more robust structure. Our advisors told us that they could provide that structure, but this didn't build family leadership because we weren't a part of that structure.

> Communication within the family wasn't robust and there wasn't a clear way of pulling it together. When the possibility of a sale came up, there was an attempt to improve communication and empower the family. But the advisors felt that their power was threatened by the sale. They were always worried about what was going to happen to them instead of working for the best interests of the family.

A sale transports the family in a new direction that they must address and adjust to:

> For a long time, our family got together because we were all connected to the company. We would meet with our advisors four times a year and meet with the company twice a year. Family board members met monthly with the board, and we had a lot of family meetings around that. We would also attend reunions, weddings, and funerals. We saw a lot of the family collectively. After the sale, we realized how important the business had been in holding us together. We try to meet quarterly but we don't have that same glue that holds us together. It's very difficult to create new things for our meetings.

RESILIENCE OF 100-YEAR FAMILY ENTERPRISES

As we will see in the following sections, a key period to build family success is after the harvest; how the family decides to regroup and recommit to new shared investments or enterprises. For many families, the business sale marks the end of the family as an organized, shared enterprise. For the generative family, it marks a turning point to a more diverse and creative future together.

"PRUNING" THE FAMILY TREE: BECOMING A FAMILY OF AFFINITY

As new members enter the family by birth and marriage, the challenge of sustaining commitment to long-term goals while sacrificing shorter-term profit distributions re-emerges as each new shareholder seeks a good return from their asset.

As the number of family owners increases, each shareholder holds a smaller share, making it more difficult to achieve alignment and shared goals. Our families adopted redemption policies that allow smaller family owners to sell their shares either back to the company or to other family members. All of the families in our study adopted **exit policies** as part of their family shareholder agreements; these policies are necessary safety valves to avoid tension around differences and destructive conflict.

In some families, different branches develop divergent interests. Some look at their business portfolio and decide to separate a long-term business with moderate risk from riskier entrepreneurial ventures. To others, owning a larger part of a smaller business can be more attractive than a small share of a larger one. Such horse trading occurs in most of our families; the development of a fair and clearly defined internal family marketplace for shareholders can sustain family ownership while allowing individuation.

In the third or fourth generation some families decide to divide their partnership by branches. When a family is so hugely successful that it owns multiple businesses or reaches a size where integration or synergy is a challenge, it may be adaptive for the family to separate branches. Several large families have gone in that direction; one member stated that it was the "village tradition" to go in separate directions as they split into several loosely connected branch portfolios. In some family traditions, the parents divide resources into separate packages for each of their children[7]. While they may miss the chance to build on a greater scale, they have their own forms of success as each family member is able to create his or her own unique destiny.

However, such arrangements need to be carefully planned. By allowing owners to exit, the family postpones the geometric rise in number and dilution of share ownership. That is why many generative businesses have a relatively small number of shareholders. Those who remain are willing to forestall current profits for longer-term goals.

Upon the sale of a legacy asset—a liquidity event—each family member has a *choice*. One option is to go their own ways with their new liquid capital. Alternately, some family members might continue to invest together by forming an investment group or family office. For example, after the sale of their huge legacy business, the largest of three family branches chose to continue as an investment group:

> *The decision to separate into three branches was organic. We'd been talking about it for a long time. The sale moved us in that direction without needing a referendum. We took a good amount of time to figure it all out. We talked to other families who have gone through similar stuff and to a lot of advisors about our options.*

---

7 This is more common outside the western world.

After the sale, family members could decide to go off on their own. This was complicated, however, because the ownership was in the trust. Ultimately, we decided to continue the trust together with new advisors and trustees. Family members had the choice to place their assets in our investment partnership.

At this point family members began to have access to stock. We have redemption policies and ways to access liquid cash. However, we want to make sure that they think through any withdrawals carefully, so we offer them resources like lawyers and accountants.

Maintaining the Vision by Pruning

Family members who are committed to the business do not want pressures for immediate dividends to trigger a sale of the business. They feel this would deprive the other family owners of the benefits of their legacy ownership. Instead, to deal with the pressures from those who want immediate returns, a generative family offers a path for individuals or a branch to sell their shares. By the fourth generation, **not one of our generative families contained all of the blood family members as shareholders.** Instead, each family offered a choice for family members to opt out of the family enterprise. (Some family trusts, however, do not allow this option.) Generative families become, as our colleague Jay Hughes observed, **families of affinity**[8]. When an exit path is offered, each family member must voluntarily decide to remain in the collective. In this way, they remain a family by choice, not blood.

This shift is especially important because family enterprises tend to limit the profit distribution to owners, preferring to reinvest in the company for the benefit of future family owners. Those who want immediate liquidity are encouraged to sell as in this example:

In our family, this reconsolidation allows family members that are not interested in the business to cash out. These members don't understand the business; they just want the highest dividends. Now they can sell their non-voting shares and do what they want with the money leaving the few who are truly committed to the business to reinvest in it. This worked well for the second and third generation. In fact, this method has been a sustainable competitive advantage for family businesses. Instead of dealing with disputes over high dividends versus reinvestment, they're able to take all that energy and focus on customers and associates.

A 5th generation Asian family had this process for reducing the number of shareholders:

If we continue letting the family tree just grow without any thought of pruning, the dilution will become too great, and we may not be able to maintain the original vision of the business. It started with my uncle, then my father had four sons and, although my father gave me a bit more of his shares, the dilution really continued. If I continue to share with my children, then each branch of the tree will become very small as we move on.

I shared my idea about tree pruning with another second-generation family business leader. I suggested to the second-generation business leader that we needed to find a way for those who want to exit the family enterprise to sell their shares. We can't turn away family members, but we can trim the number of shareholders by allowing them to cash in their shares. Then only those who are more passionate about the business will remain as the shareholders. As we move to the fifth generation, we may have to do another pruning.

8 Our work is much influenced by Jay's work. His most recent offering, **Complete Family Wealth** (James Hughes, Susan Massenzio and Keith Whitaker, Bloomberg Press, 2017), presents the concept of family of affinity and many others.

RESILIENCE OF 100-YEAR FAMILY ENTERPRISES

Some business families face another kind of liquidity event: the dissolution of a trust. Most trusts have an ending date, but when they are set up, the ending date may be generations away, so there is little consideration of what the date means. However, when that date actually approaches, the beneficiaries of the trust need to make a choice about how the trust's assets will be held in the future. They must decide whether they want to remain together and, if they do, how to invest the money. Here's how one family dealt with this issue:

> Each branch had significant assets and trusts. Eventually those trusts would break, so the question was how do we keep people engaged together? What happens when people have the freedom to leave? In 1995, the sixth generation gathered for the first time. Three of us fifth generation leaders asked them to help develop a strategic plan for the trust company. We began to anticipate what would happen next.

"DIVERSIFYING" FROM SINGLE BUSINESS TO PORTFOLIO

The evolution from owner/managers of a legacy business to managing a portfolio of businesses often arises when a new generation of young leaders begins to take over. This generation arrives with new energy, top-notch business educations, apprenticeships, and commitment to the family. They may see challenges ahead for the legacy business and investigate possible ways to renew it, reinvest, expand, or take on other investors. For example, liquidity from ESOPS (employee stock ownership programs) might allow some family members to cash out. Conversely, offering stock to key family executives or advisors might enable them to reinvest in the company. Family owners may then seek opportunities to buy another business or engage in shared investments within a family office or private trust company. These families discover many opportunities. They may be large enough to create an internal economy in which different family members can invest in certain projects, each with different degrees of cross-family ownership.

After selling the legacy business, a business family has a rare opportunity to regroup and redefine itself. This opens the door to new entrepreneurial ventures by the family. Here's how one family created a new enterprise:

> Now, we don't have a fancy public family business. We have a tightly run, profitable business that provides investment opportunities available nowhere else. Our real estate department operates at a 99% occupancy rate. We have malls, apartment buildings, and offices. The trust management looks after the partners of a private capital fund with nine different managers across a variety of disciplines including venture capital. All this provides opportunities for each generation. Although we don't have a visible business any more, we don't want to lose these opportunities for future generations. We hope for new entrepreneurialism and new invention.

While the older generation and professional managers may tend toward a conservative approach and risk avoidance, the emergence of a rising generation with a desire for innovation can move the family in a more entrepreneurial direction. The entrepreneurial energy of the new generation can challenge and balance the conservatism of the older generation and the professional business leaders. The family needs to engage these talented young people after they have developed capability and credibility but before they are fully established outside the family orbit. The family also has to initiate checks and balances on investments and new ideas so the enthusiasm and desire for risk by the younger generation is balanced by prudence. However, the older generation cannot be too conservative. One family missed the opportunity to invest early on in one of the Internet pioneers. The younger generation presented the idea passionately and thoughtfully, but the family was not willing to take the risk.

HOW OPPORTUNISTIC INNOVATION, BUSINESS DISCIPLINE, AND A CULTURE OF STEWARDSHIP GUIDE THE JOURNEY ACROSS GENERATIONS

A European manufacturing business went through this evolution. As described below, two generations had to work through their differences:

The company rose from our single operating family business into a financial holding company with a family office. We needed to diversify and shift our focus beyond our industry in Europe. There were a number of issues that were hotly debated between the third and fourth generations. Should we sell the business? If we sold, how should we invest the proceeds? Should we invest in more diverse holdings, or should we distribute the proceeds to the shareholders?

Financing had become more difficult. If we went to the bank, we were offered higher rates, so we decided to separate the export activities in Africa from the core company and set up a holding company at the top. Some non-involved family members were allowed to separate themselves from the core activities. This was a positive thing because it allowed the managers to make decisions without needing to get input from these members.

This report from a middle-eastern conglomerate typifies the organization of non-US family ventures that have diversified into many parts:

The family holding company used to be comprised exclusively of family shareholders: these shareholders held either 100% or a majority stake in all of our businesses. But last year, for the first time, we took a minority stake in one of our own SBUs because it required such a heavy investment (it was a supermarket chain). Outside investors put in money; now we're 49% and they're 51%.

A family enterprise can contain both public and private business entities. They may be combined into a family holding company as was done by this fifth-generation European conglomerate:

On the private side, we have a holding company which is the original company. This now amounts to about 50% of the public company. The public company has four economic drivers: a power utility, a commercial bank, a consumer goods company, and real estate. All of these are public, but the private holding company holds a big chunk of the public company. We now have a market cap of about seven billion dollars.

A family with a legacy business dating back more than a century started a family partnership outside their public company. This partnership had a family advisory board and two family member executives who joined the business after working for venture capital and financial firms. Their venture capital investments fit the interests of their rising generation and were supported by the capability of experienced family and non-family leaders.

Managing the portfolio can represent a challenge to the family, as this European company learned when they crossed generations:

In 2009, we had a liquidity event: we sold part of the farming company. This enabled us to buy out my grandfather, so he could retire in peace. We also had funds to buy out the generation of my father and my uncle. However, this raised a lot of disagreements. Some people wanted to sell the company, while others were absolutely against it. It was a very difficult time involving many arduous and heated discussions.

Eventually, the majority of the family agreed to sell the company. This was a momentous decision because it was our core business. Next, we reached an agreement with the older generation about a generational transition. Ultimately, we were able to buy out the elders, and we ended 2009 with my generation in control of the family council.

RESILIENCE OF 100-YEAR FAMILY ENTERPRISES

Moving to a portfolio also allows for differences in the type of family leadership. Instead of a single leader, the family might develop multiple leaders with different skills who manage different types of assets. Some families, especially those outside the US, allow family members to acquire and manage different businesses. However, the portfolio needs a central holding company or board of directors that can manage the interaction of all of the assets together. The legacy company may have had a single family leader in the previous generation; the shift to a portfolio opens the door for shared leadership by family members who can oversee different areas. Instead of a single leader, a board, investment committee, or special task force can diversify the family investments.

STORY #2: ADOPTING AN ENTREPRENEURIAL MINDSET FOR THE FAMILY PORTFOLIO

In generative families, taking prudent risks and adopting new directions often win over the more conservative elements of the family. As an example, after selling the legacy business, this rising generation found the opportunity to influence the new family direction:

At the beginning, of course, we were just one single operating unit. Later, when the operation started generating enough cash, we began to diversify. We created our own diverse portfolio to have as a security blanket if something happened to the core business. This has been a continuous strategy; it's never been set aside or forgotten. And we've always continued to increase our portfolio.

After a time, we felt uneasy because we were doing so many things at the same time without a strategy to tie them all together. We were missing opportunities. Now that we've moved to a holding company, we have an overview of all the businesses, and we can interrelate each business. This enables us to prepare strategies for sales, production, and growth for each business. We can also create synergies among the various businesses.

The goal of the holding company is to continue to purchase more companies and create more opportunities, always with a clear strategy. Two months from now, we're going to have the first consolidated statement for the entire group.

We all have an entrepreneurial mindset, an excitement about creating new business opportunities. It's challenging and exciting and a lot of fun. This spirit comes from the family mission, our way of looking at life. We're never satisfied with the status quo. The lessons we learned from our upbringing have made us reach for continuous movement and change.

We sometimes feel the need to settle what we have before we look for new things. But every time we say that, something new comes along, and everybody gets very excited. There's always somebody looking for something. We have a very solid liquid investment portfolio, and that makes for peace of mind as we move ahead.

"GROUNDING." FAMILY OFFICES AS CENTERS FOR GOVERNANCE AND FAMILY IDENTITY

All over the world, we see a dramatic growth in the number of entities called family offices. After the success of a family business, the family might begin to accumulate wealth from other assets. A "liquidity" event like the sale of all or part of a family business or the accumulation of capital from the profits of the business creates the need for the family to manage assets and investments outside the business. At first, if the business is privately-held, the other assets can be managed from within the business. But if there are other shareholders or the business is sold or goes public, the financial affairs of the extended family will need to be managed separately.

A family office provides new services to a family, including tax filing and legal compliance, financial advising, wealth portfolio management, support for family lifestyles, administration of trusts, and estate planning. The location of these services outside the legacy business creates what is called a family office. If the family has a large amount of capital or multiple assets, the office can be quite large and contain a large professional staff. In effect, it becomes another business owned by the family that must be governed. Forming a family office after the sale of a legacy business creates a new center for the identity and shared engagement of the family apart from their business. A family has to decide whether they want their own office, or whether they want to join with other families and receive these services through a multi-family office, trust company, or financial firm.

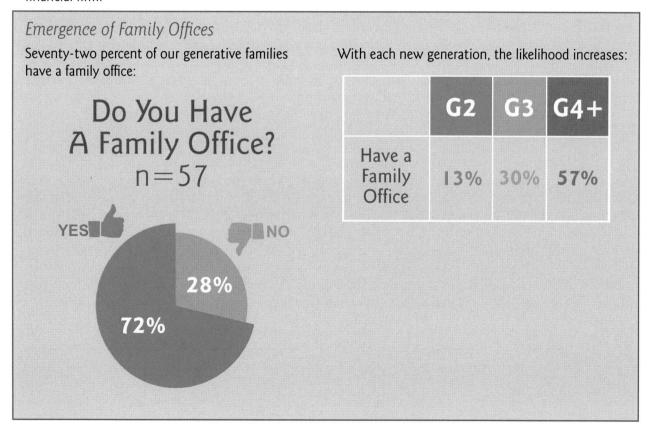

Emergence of Family Offices

Seventy-two percent of our generative families have a family office:

Do You Have A Family Office? n=57

YES 72% NO 28%

With each new generation, the likelihood increases:

	G2	G3	G4+
Have a Family Office	13%	30%	57%

RESILIENCE OF 100-YEAR FAMILY ENTERPRISES

In the third generation, only a third of our families had a family office. By the fourth generation, 57% of our families had one. Forming a family office is often not a clear decision at a single point in time but may evolve as the family requires attention to taxes, investments, personal expenses, philanthropy, and shared family activities outside the business. While this makes the governance more complex, a family office enables the family to remain together as an organized, value-creating entity.

A family office may be created after the sale of a large business as described here:

> *We have an investment management committee that recommends certain investments—and we do a bit of our own research. We also have a family office with a very small staff. We have experts in investments, legal matters, philanthropy, and tax preparation. For some things, like tax prep, we might pay a little bit more, but we feel that we're getting the latest and greatest strategies.*

As with other types of family business, the family exercises control over their assets. They have values about investments, and they want to sustain their identity as a family. Moving away from a single legacy business, the family office becomes the heart and soul of the family, the place where the family efforts are centered. If there is a family council, a board, family activity for education, a family vacation home, or support for individual households, the family office is where all these things are coordinated. Providing these family-related services is sometimes seen as worth the extra cost.

The family office contains assets beyond the legacy business. Acquiring additional assets allows the family to diversify; this lessens the risk of owning just a single huge asset. The diversified family office might include a trust, a holding company, an LLP, a private trust company, or other forms of partnership. It is governed by a board or trustees separate from the board of the legacy company. Family members can be board members, owners, staff, or CEO of these entities. They make the "business" pillar of family governance a sort of double pillar as the family office grows alongside the legacy business. Family conglomerates have complex structures that may own several large investments and companies. The goals of the family office are to preserve and grow assets, build a diverse array of businesses, and act as a center for other family activities.

Why do generative families often prefer single family offices rather than being part of a shared multi-family group (a less expensive alternative)? This is because in addition to the financial services, the family office acts as a clubhouse and community center for the extended family. If the family is not widely dispersed, the family office has even more value to the family. In visiting family offices, one often finds a museum of family artifacts and a long-serving staff who are close to family members and are available to assist them with issues and concerns. Members can get help not only with tax and financial issues, but also relationship and personal issues that arise in the family. Family office staff can help negotiate pre-nuptial agreements and divorces, assist in buying houses, boats, planes, and art, and attend to safety and security. There are places for family meetings to be held and places to store and keep family records. The office embodies the family's identity and commitments.

To allow the family to act as its own trustee for a family trust, a complex, highly-regulated bank-like entity called a **private trust company** can be created. For example, a family that owned and controlled a large public company began to diversify by selling stock in the business. They needed a home for these new investments, and they wanted to consolidate the investments that were held in various institutions and trusts. They could justify the expense of setting up a private trust company because they wanted to be actively involved in investment decisions using the wisdom of their talented fourth generation.

As a family accumulates wealth, they often want to invest as a family according to their legacy values. They see opportunities to combine their values with their investments. However, some family members may not share these values, or want to invest in other ways. The solution to this conflict lies in allowing family members to cash out. Many families report that when they set up their family office, they offer family branches and members the option to exit and take their money out., and also an opportunity to initiate a new period of growth or redefine their business and investment values.

Additional Functions for Family Offices

Larger families have more complex needs for their family offices. They may have farming, ranch, and vacation properties that need active oversight and other natural resources with complex regulations and tax implications. In addition, they may have venture capital arms with active or passive investments, concerns about impact and social responsibility, philanthropic arms that oversee foundation assets and the foundation itself, and other personal investments by family members. The family office might manage investments and personal affairs of many individual households. For example, when they sold the legacy business, a four-branch family split the proceeds. The largest branch formed a family office and moved into new investment areas, but this new family office served only 16 of the 64 family members.

These family offices might create a new board that sets up various task groups. One such task group might be an investment committee to manage the family investments. Other families might have small internal offices and outsource the investment management to other financial advisors. The emerging functions of the family office allow the expression of innovation and entrepreneurial impulses, as the enterprise moves in new directions.

RESILIENCE OF 100-YEAR FAMILY ENTERPRISES

Taking Action In Your Own Family Enterprise

Every multi-generational family enterprise has experienced major transformations like the Big Four (harvesting, pruning, diversifying and grounding) that we talked about in this section. In addition, they can look ahead and anticipate the need for any of them in the future. Success in your family journey depends upon how well prepared you are when the event occurs and how well you re-align and re-define your family in response to it.

As you think about each of the major transformations, reflect on when they took place in your family. For each one, consider the three stages of preparing for change. You can start by answering these questions:

● Has your family gone through any of these major shifts?

● Do you anticipate the need for any of them in the coming years?

You might then conduct an assessment of how you managed the transformations that your family has experienced. This assessment can be done from the perspective of preserving family connection and business adaptability as well as what you might have done to improve your handling of the changes.

	HARVESTING	PRUNING	DIVERSIFYING	GROUNDING
Prepare Anticipate				
Engage Decide				
Defefine Renew				

It's never too late to set in motion positive measures to make your family change-ready in the future. Toward that end, you might want to look ahead at possible major changes and consider how your family is anticipating and preparing for them.

Part Four – Building a Resilient Culture for Business Evolution

A generative family continually develops, sustains, extends, and redefines itself as it passes through the major transformations described in the previous section. But there is always a consistent and enduring core: the legacy values and ways of doing business that make up its identity as a business family. While each family is unique, several broad but consistent patterns make up the cultural DNA of the generative family. These patterns enable the family to develop disciplined, professional businesses while retaining the ability to adapt and renew. The unique generative family culture we uncovered combines and blends the developmental paths of both the Craftsman and the Opportunist.

Unlike many public businesses, the culture of a multi-generational family business is enduring and consistent. A strong, well-defined culture defines in a predictable way what they stand for—their values, practices, and ways of doing things. A clear and strong culture creates trust between family and non-family stakeholders as well as with customers, suppliers, and the entire community in which it does business. It makes public and explicit that the family owners stand for more than short-term profit. This commitment is usually clearly and publicly stated, so if there is a breach or even a perceived breach, it can be challenged.

Each of our generative families developed a strong and well-defined **family culture** consisting of values about family, wealth, and the purpose of the family enterprise. This culture does not emerge all at once. It begins with the legacy values and actions of the business/family founders, then evolves as the family renews and develops itself in each new generation. While each family's culture is distinctive with a different personal style and flavor based on its personal origins, there are consistencies across generative cultures. Culture forms the major pathway for the expression of the adaptive capability of the generative alliance. Culture has consistencies across generations, but each new generation of a family enterprise also renews the family commitment and often adopts or revises elements of the culture.

SIX CULTURAL THEMES

Six themes are common to almost all the families in our study. Taken together, their presence differentiates generative families from enduring but less successful family enterprises. Because family owners also have a history, legacy, and personal relationship to each other and their business, their values, goals, and operating principles are more extensive than those of owners who simply desire a good financial return.

Researchers[9] view this family-based culture as a competitive advantage held by family enterprises over public companies that do not have family oversight. It has been defined as *"familiness,"* meaning the family-based resources and qualities arising from family control and ownership. These six themes are clearly linked to aspects of the generative stakeholder alliance:

---

9 The insight that the resources developed by positive family relationships, values, skills, and shared purpose can be a source of competitive advantage and account in a positive way for the success of special families like the ones we write about over many generations has been developed by researchers Danny Miller and Isabel Le Breton-Miller in **Managing for the Long Run** (Harvard Business School Press, 2005), and T. G. Habbershon and M.L. Williams, *A resource-based framework for assessing the strategic advantage of family firms* (**Family Business Review,** Vol 12, No 1, 1999). They present the view that we have validated in our work, that while family relationships can surely be destructive of a business, when aligned and used wisely, they can add significant value to the success and adaptability of an enterprise.

Elements of Family Culture Supporting Family Enterprise

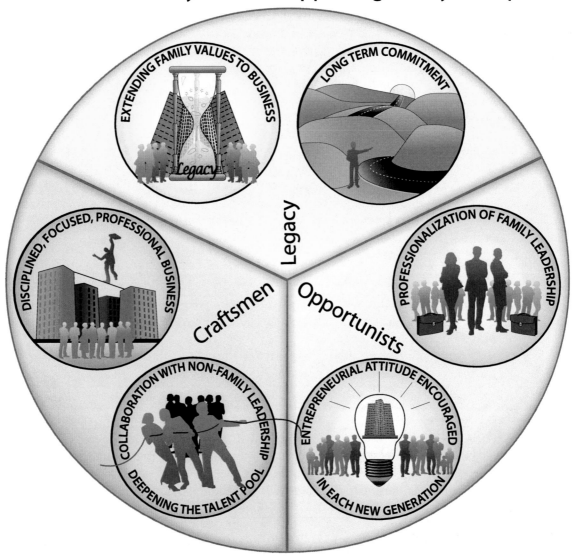

The family enterprise culture is made up of contributions derived from the three core elements of the **Generative Family Alliance.** Shared legacy values along with different perspectives and skills combine to create a resilient and adaptive culture. This culture can be contrasted with the more short-term and transactional culture of many non-family businesses. The elder generation promotes and supports a long-term commitment to the shared enterprises and passes that down to their heirs. They also pass on their values that are expressed in how the business operates, its products, and its role in the community. The elders and many of their family and non-family allies, holding the craftsmen orientation, take steps to develop a professional business operation by recruiting and collaborating with professional business leaders outside the family. As the younger generation grows up and appreciates their legacy, they add their own adaptive, entrepreneurial thrust to the direction of the family enterprise.

LONG TERM COMMITMENT

Generative family enterprises are not looking for immediate profit or short-term gains; they are there for the long-term. As stewards, they look more than a generation ahead for the benefit of their children. This engenders patience as they develop the values, skills, and resources of each new generation to contribute to the growth and development of the enterprises. Without such patience and thoughtful preparation, success would be hard to repeat and sustain.

Time fuels the drive of generative families across generations. Their attention is always focused ahead—on future generations and the future of their business. They make significant investments in the business and look ahead for opportunities. They exercise what has been termed "patient capital" for return on their investments. As a European family elder observes:

> By definition, if you are thinking about the next generation, not just the next quarter, that's another 25 years. You want the story to continue; that's deeply rooted in all family businesses. That long-term perspective is very, very important. This is reflected in the HR policies of the company; the employees know that you are in for a lot more than just making money.

Long-term commitment has many advantages, the most common being freedom to take on major projects without worrying about short-term losses or disaffected shareholders. They are able to exercise patience to see results. This attitude extends from the family into the values of the business culture, as these two families observe:

> Family 1: I think the single biggest advantage is the long-term horizon. I don't worry about the month or the quarter or the year, I worry about whether everything we do is going to help us to be in business for another 100 years. More than anything else, that's what I like about being here. The other thing is nepotism has an extremely bad name; it has a negative connotation. But we've found it to be extremely positive because of all the brothers, sisters, uncles, and cousins of our non-family employees that bring their families into the business. We have families that have more than 200 years of service over four generations of uncles, sisters and brothers. The family culture has expanded to all employees, and we have just about zero turnover. We have a guy in our electronic department that has 68 years of service. In the 25 years I've been here, we've had eight people retire with 50 years of service or more.

> Family 2: It's an advantage being private because you can make long-term decisions and be very diverse. For example, we have recently gone into two of the huge mines—a high-risk investment. If we were a listed company, the shareholders would say, "What the hell are you doing?" But we can diversify into industries we like. We're also quite counter-cyclical. If the property market's completely dead, we'll double down. If the property market's heated, we'll start selling.

This commitment comes from the entire family, as a member of one such family expresses:

> The family has a very strong sense of pride and ownership of the company, so there is a reluctance to sell any shares or liquidate their interests. Their sense is, "I want to pass this down to my children and grandchildren and let them be part of what our grandfathers created."

This commitment is not to a single business, but to a shared cross-generational partnership and values reflected in everything the family does. The family can sell the business and remain together as a business family. The sale offers an opportunity for some family members to go their own ways but enables the rest to become an entirely new kind of business entity. Their culture and values are then transferred to new ventures or shared investments.

RESILIENCE OF 100-YEAR FAMILY ENTERPRISES

This commitment is not a one-time choice but must be affirmed regularly by the family, because it demands so much of them. With every generation, each family must answer the question: **Do we want to stay together?** Sometimes they decide that "the business would have a better future without the family, and we would have a better future without the business." Unless the family is willing to make a substantial time commitment to overseeing the enterprise, it is not to their advantage to remain owners.

Going into its seventh generation, a natural resources business evolved into a **family conglomerate** with dozens of operating businesses. These had been acquired with the engagement of an entire family assembly as an advisory voice. The family CEO of this group observes:

> *The challenge is making sure that we're renewing our wealth, so we can continue to support a growing family. Some of our recent business decisions focused on how we are going to get to 2030. How can we build a business that can provide us with the income we need to fund family programs and annual meetings? That's very different from the way most businesses would look at such things; it's really looking long term versus short term. At the same time, you have to put money into the shareholder's pockets, so you're obligated to provide liquidity on an annual basis. It's a huge challenge to create liquidity in a private company.*

Long-term commitment also represents a dependable personal commitment to respect loyal service to the family. One European conglomerate has several family managing directors who oversee the various enterprises. They say that family members who work in the business "die with their boots on." No one has ever left. When the current family CEO took the job, he did so understanding that it would be his last job. He's most proud of the fact that the family members in the business live no differently than their one thousand employees. He's proud of the loyalty and mutual respect that they've cultivated both with employees and with hundreds of family owners.

EXTENDING FAMILY VALUES INTO BUSINESS

The meaning of "family" in a family enterprise extends beyond blood family to include employees, suppliers, customers, and the community. This explains their ability to engender commitment and inspire performance and shared purpose. Facilitative values about how family owners do business have been instilled in the culture from Day One. They continue because, even as business leadership passes outside the family, the culture reflects, reinforces, and stands for these values. As the family becomes a *family of affinity*, there is room for long-time employees and advisors to take on quasi-family roles and status.

With a long-term focus, the family creates an environment in which employees can depend on the family to be there for them and their children. It acts as the foundation for the corporate culture and values that influences all decisions as described below:

> *We always show that our local roots matter. Employees in China or India understand that they are also part of this local history. When they come and visit the homeland, they are very proud too. To give an example, for several years things were very difficult, and the family didn't take any dividends. We told our workers, "You know, even though we put all our money in, we had to put more in, and we don't take dividends." They said, "We just have to power through." All the little traditions make everyone feel involved, like the firm's own music band or the Christmas tree from the firm's forests. These things make them say proudly, "Yes, I work here!"*

> *Our business has always been long term because you always have to calculate your risks in relation to how long you want it to go on. It's quite unusual to see family businesses willing to bet everything on the short term even though sometimes there can be exceptional rewards. You have to remember that you have the responsibility for all those people that make the product. That's a lot of lives, and that makes the responsibility even heavier.*

Employees are important, respected, and have equal standing to family employees and the owner. When a family clearly states its values, it creates trust that people outside the family depend on. Of course, these expressed values must be backed by policies and action that are congruent with them. In generative family cultures talk and action are clearly connected. A family member with a profitable business notes:

> *Our culture is that employees are treated like family. We created an ESOP (Employee Stock Ownership Plan) so employees could share in the profits. Family owners receive very small dividends. The message is that key employees who actively produce value for the business take precedence over family financial rewards. If family members want to convert their ownership to cash, they can redeem stock every year. But selling stock is a costly and consequential decision that family members do not take lightly.*

This statement by a non-family CEO defines the qualities for a professionally-run, values-based family enterprise that give them a competitive advantage over a public company:

> *As managers, executives, employees, and staff, the number one focus is always on family, whether it's the client's family or the employees' families. We make sure that employees are able to care for their own families. If you've got things happening at your kid's school in the middle of the day, whether you are a file clerk or an accountant you should be able to be there without having to take time off. Allowing people to be at their family events conveys the importance of family. Because they're aware of the attention given to their families, everyone here wants to work hard. People are generally here for a very long time. Most of our employees give over 20 years of service.*

> *I can't say enough positive things about the family I work with. In 2008, when the world was falling apart financially, many family offices were deciding, "No raises or bonuses this year. It's a bad year, so we can't really do this." For us, the discussion that took place with employees was, Are you telling me that even though this has happened, the family that we represent is not going to feel the impact of this? I mean, it's not going to change their life in any way? So, what about all the families that work for you? They're absolutely affected by this. If you're only being great leaders at times when things are solid and strong, what does this say? The reality is, we should look at our employees and say, "You need a bigger increase than normal to help you get through this downturn." We made sure everybody received the equivalent to help them through the financial strife. That showed true strength in their leadership and why the idea of family is at the core of everything.*

One family has a strong values statement passed down by the founder that is taught to each employee. The values are emphasized in hiring and each employee is expected to adhere to them. When this family acquired a much larger division of a public company with a very different culture and values, they made a clear offer to employees of that division: "You are welcome to join us, but we expect that you will adhere to our values." To their surprise, most employees of the acquired company chose to stay.

Family values about employees are particularly important when the company is challenged by a crisis. When the pressure is on, employees want to know where they stand and whether the family will continue to honor their values. One family was on the verge of selling their three-generation family manufacturing business. It was deeply rooted in their community but was facing cost pressures to move manufacturing overseas. A private capital firm approached to buy the company. They were close to the sale when the family realized that there was deep resistance on the part of their employees and customers. Ultimately, they decided to not sell and instead hired a non-family CEO. A family spokesperson stated:

> *The customers were not happy that we were selling the business, nor were our employees. They saw the value of the family's policies in pricing, product quality, and timeliness of delivery. Although it's never been explicitly stated, this is why all of these things work so well and pricing is competitive. They could pick up the phone and call my dad if something went wrong.*

> *There's the high touch factor in a family business that is important to customers. We're exploring this with our new CEO, how do we use that factor to our advantage, now that we've decided to remain family owned for the next generation? How do we use that and create a story around it? The story is that we're a professionally run family business, but we have strong family values and want to hold onto our very special culture.*

Another view of the extent of this commitment to employees and community is expressed by a fifth-generation family leader. This view—known as the "stakeholder" view—holds that the family has a moral obligation to serve different communities. This stakeholder philosophy stands in marked contrast to the view that the only responsibility of a business is to generate profit for shareholders. In recent years, many public companies have learned from the example of family enterprise by adopting this view of their corporate responsibility. As this quote illustrates, in this view, families see their obligations as owners much more broadly:

> *Responsibility to the company sometimes lies above the shareholders. Especially in this small town, where we are one of the major employers, the success of this company is all important. Our commitment to our employees makes for a kind of shared value and a dedication to make the company a success. If we focused only on our shareholders, that would be the death of the business.*

A DISCIPLINED, FOCUSED, PROFESSIONAL BUSINESS

Whatever values are held by a family, each family enterprise is a business intended to be profitable. The family's values and entrepreneurial attitudes have to be housed within a sustainable, professional, disciplined, focused, and competent business. The first-generation business founder may have been an improvisational leader, often operating without a design or plan, moving forward on opportunities, taking risks, and making gut decisions. As successive generations enter leadership, however, they face the challenge of adding conventional business practices and discipline. They cannot continue to run on improvisational family leadership; they have to recruit and develop skilled non-family leaders who share the family's values and long-term commitment. This in itself can bring about a profound transformation of the business, but each of our generative families were able to accomplish this while sustaining the family's connection and values. This was a major developmental hurdle for them.

HOW OPPORTUNISTIC INNOVATION, BUSINESS DISCIPLINE, AND A CULTURE OF STEWARDSHIP GUIDE THE JOURNEY ACROSS GENERATIONS

Somewhere between the second and fourth generations, family leadership transitions to a professional focus. The leaders must exercise the skills of the **craftsman** while developing business discipline, professional operations, and accountability. This is a critical point for a generative family as they attempt to deal with these questions:

● How do we attract managers and leaders whose competence extends beyond that of the family?

● Will our oversight as owners embody and demand professional standards and practices?

● Can our vision and culture be extended beyond the family?

● What must change about our company and the way we do business?

For the family, this transition involves coming to terms with the reality that the business needs come before the family. The family must look outside itself, to the strength and vicability of the business, before they attend their own needs. Rather than see business as an arena for meeting family needs, the family now sees the business as a delicate resource that needs professional care to be sustained. This means moving from an improvisational, informal practices to moving toward creating a business culture that focuses recruiting and organizing an excellent business. The care and perfectionism of the craftsman must replace the family's natural tendency to see the business as their playground.

Since this shift involves less skilled and professional family members giving up jobs, perks, and influence, it almost never takes place without stress, conflict, and drama. There can be a painful family rift as a dedicated but less professional family leader is asked to leave, and the family learns to respect and defer to non-family leaders on operational issues.

This transfer in a European family enterprise was stressful but effective:

> For the first few generations, power was handed over from father to son, from strong character to the next strong character. It was the responsibility of the people in place to nurture and select the next leaders. In my father's generation, several family members were involved in executive management positions.

> There was friction when appointed family leaders had to be removed; this was a painful exercise. This is one of the reasons why we said that in the next generation, we would no longer allow family involvement in management. In addition, we wanted to give our professional managers the opportunity to rise to the highest executive levels. This meant that family members would no longer be first in line for leadership positions.

Professionalizing the business is often accompanied by diversification. This can provide the opportunity for family members to redefine their individual ventures. Some households or branches may decide they want to go off in their own directions, as in this Asian family:

> My family has one third-generation family business and my own first-generation company. I started thinking that I should play my part in moving the family business towards professional management. We needed to transform from a business family to an investment family. I decided to build an investment portfolio, so my children could leverage on my own family business. I believe that each generation should create their own wealth instead of depending on the ancestors' business. I expect my children to have different interests; I don't believe in forcing them to pick up my grandfather's business or even my business.

RESILIENCE OF 100-YEAR FAMILY ENTERPRISES

I would like my children to be good shareholders in my grandfather's business and in my own business, but I would also like them to create their own sole ventures. I envision each child having his own enterprise that emerges from his own vision.

Sometimes the impetus to change comes from the marketplace. When they moved to Europe, this Middle Eastern business family had to adapt to external change and redefine their very personal, hands-on business:

The 1970s to early '90s in Europe were the heydays of the luxury business; there were lots of Middle Eastern families coming to Europe. The family was good at negotiating with them because they themselves were from the Middle East. They knew a bit about the mind-set and cultural mores of their clients and adapted very well to their needs and attitudes. But the growth was chaotic. The family never bothered to clarify how they would organize the business.

The business model was essentially a trading model: buy cheap, sell expensive. This was successful until the early '90s, but at that time two things happened. One was the first Gulf War when the key customer base stopped buying. The second was competition; the luxury business started attracting a lot of competition because margins were high. Large luxury groups entered our sector. At this point we had to become more professional and competent in management, but we didn't know how to do that. The family couldn't imagine getting competent outsiders to help us out. They couldn't even imagine how to clarify their own functioning or make compromises about their prerogatives and powers.

When I joined the management team eight years ago, my very first job was to write contracts and job descriptions for everybody. It was tough for the family to accept these contracts. Even the employees resisted—they were used to oral commands. Nobody wanted things formalized; they didn't want to take the time to write things out.

A member of a large family food manufacturer transitioning from third to fourth generation, discusses how this difficult transformation was introduced and managed:

Seven years ago, we said: "Let's be a little bit more intentional and say that family is family and business is business. We started to go through a transition, moving from a family business to a business family. When you have a family business, employment becomes a birthright. This meant that we were getting too many family members into the business who weren't qualified, and performance was suffering. For a family business, the primary goal is to maintain family harmony; profits are secondary. By contrast, the business family focuses on business first; profits are respected and expected, and performance comes first. This means getting qualified people in the right places throughout the business. We went from focusing on family harmony to business performance; this was a really hard thing for us to do. We started that journey back in 2000, and we've been on that track ever since with a tremendous growth in business performance.

While we noticed that sales had dramatically increased over the years, some problems remained the same. Because of our Christian heritage, we believed the reason the company existed was so that the family could contribute to charities. Sales were growing, but profits remained flat and people started asking, "How come we don't have as much money to give away? What's going on?" A group from the older generation examined our options. All options were on the table including keeping the business, selling the business, or restructuring it. All family branches were involved, and the vote had to be unanimous. In the end, we decided that the right thing to do was to sustain this business for future generations.

HOW OPPORTUNISTIC INNOVATION, BUSINESS DISCIPLINE, AND A CULTURE OF STEWARDSHIP GUIDE THE JOURNEY ACROSS GENERATIONS

When a business transitions to non-family leadership, the family is often unsure about their role. When this European family conglomerate shifted to professional management, they had to learn a new role for family leadership:

> When we adopted professional management, the biggest challenge facing the fourth generation was discovering new ways for the family to lead. They were being overshadowed by the experience professionals on the executive team, but after three years they are finally on the case and contributing. One thing G4 accomplished was to begin to formulate strategic superordinate goals to present to the group board for discussion. For example, one goal is to see 25 percent of income come from the housing market. We wanted a balanced business with strong values, but we had to learn to spell out these values definitively—to move the input from the family into the business strategy.

Business discipline can entail challenging non-performing family leaders. Easing out non-performing leaders is a challenge for any business but more so for a business family as this account illustrates:

> My uncle and my dad will always remember when they opened a new department led by an older uncle. There was a big emotional aspect there. This business had losses for many, many years; it finally got so bad that we had to close it. But the decision created a lot of conflict because my uncle's identity was so wrapped up in it. It was hard to tell him that he had to leave.

> This situation led the family to decide to professionalize management. Everybody agreed to shift to a formal, objective selection process for anyone in the family who wanted to work in the family business. This led us in turn to move towards governance structures that diversified the risk and to create a holding system that managed family cash flow. In addition, we had to establish shareholder agreements. We had a large minority group that wanted more transparency, feasibility, and objectivity with professional management and independent directors on the board. All this led us to our current structure.

Another European beverage business, many generations old, made a similar shift in their sixth generation:

> When I was on the board, we made a big change eight years ago. The company needed to be professionalized and shift to a more global outlook. This process was not easy, but we are proud that we did it in a safe, gentle way.

> How do things get handled when jealousy emerges because some family members get certain privileges that others don't have? Even though these may not be huge privileges, they still upset other members of the family. To avoid these conflicts, we decided that only four family members will work in the company.

Sometimes the transition to non-family leadership arises when the family doesn't have a candidate for leadership:

> The shift away from operating ownership wasn't a conscious decision. Nobody in the family wanted to do it. My son was in there for a while and he got out. My nephew was in there and he got out, but there wasn't another family member to take the spot. So that's when the shift to leaders outside the family happened. Some very able people came along in the next generation, however, and I'm having regrets that no family member is in the operations now.

RESILIENCE OF 100-YEAR FAMILY ENTERPRISES

Having a culture of business accountability reassures employees that family needs and practices will not push aside performance, respect for employee professionalism, and appropriate rewards. The value of long-term business success overrides immediate family needs. For generative families, there is usually a transition where the long-term orientation of the family area applied to reviewing business policies and raising the expectations for the business not just to do what the family wants but to conduct itself in accord with principles of quality, accountability and fair policies that are characteristic of "excellent" companies.

DEEPENING THE TALENT POOL:
COLLABORATING WITH NON-FAMILY LEADERSHIP

After one or two generations where family owners are also hands-on business operators, the family reaches a point where the family talent pool cannot encompass all the needs of their various enterprises. At this point, the family must consider where they will find next generation business leaders. Family members might continue to work in the business, but employment is no longer linked to eventual business leadership. As we see in the following section, family oversight moves to the board and the governance entities that oversee the businesses.

At this point, family members can no longer assume that their businesses are potential places of employment where they can come and go as they please. Individual family members, or a whole branch, may then choose to give up their ownership and are bought out. The new professional enterprise now has a different relationship with the family. At this time, family members often set up other business, financial, and philanthropic ventures, and begin to practice family governance. Some family members take on the opportunistic path, while others support the craftsmanship orientation.

The family increasingly looks to recruit and collaborate with non-family leaders who share the family's values and support its unique culture but add further skills and capability. As they begin to lead the family's businesses, family office, investments, and foundations, they work closely with emerging family leaders who are not in operations, especially the rising generation. The shift away from being family owner/operators while still sustaining the family culture and values is a critical transition for the generative family.

Business founders are notoriously secretive. They often don't trust their employees and are reluctant to share financial data even with family members. However, to build a culture of accountability and professional practice, the family must overcome its habit of not sharing information. As new generations emerge in generative families, the cultural value of openness and transparency overcomes the founder's tendency to restrict information and distrust of others. As this account illustrates, transparency can evolve in the culture of the business:

> *Up to the early 70s, accounting was done in a dark room where the numbers were kept away from everyone. But starting with my father's generation, we began to rely on computers, data, and formal statements and began the process of professionalizing the ERP. Now that factual data is shared with managers, we all know how we're doing. At board meetings, we go through everything in great detail; when we went public, it was easy for us to make a transition because we were already there.*

When the business faces pressures, the family feels an obligation to explain impending changes. This is part of their commitment to transparency. They explain what they are doing and why with the employees, and this creates an alignment and shared purpose. Here's how one business accomplishes this:

We also are doing a roadshow this year. The CEO and I (the Chair) are going to all the sites around the world to talk about what the family is doing in terms of the transition. Everyone knows that the CEO is reaching retirement, and we want to make sure that we're closing the circle in terms of communication.

As they age, the older generation experiences a diminished ability to lead the business. They lose energy and access to new ideas and opportunities. They get stale, but they are often the last to see this. Sometimes that task is taken up by the new generation; they may need to confront the existing powers in order to sustain the business. A fourth-generation daughter observes:

I feel a very strong divide between the third and the fourth generations. The third generation is much less open to change. The only way change can happen is by a buyout of the third generation's moral symbolic stake in the business. This can happen by their leaving the business either by dying, retiring, or going to Norway to fish salmon. There has to be agreement among successors and the incumbent generation about what it is being done, where the business is going, and what kind of changes the previous generation might be open to.

How does agreement that change is needed evolve? In this family, the daughter's father was pressed into service when his father died suddenly when he was young. He was unprepared and wanted to ensure that this never happened to his children. Early on, his daughter demonstrated skills that complemented those of the next generation's successor from the other side of the family. After consultation with her father and siblings, she asked for the position. They created a timeline and a training process that involved graduate school, work in other businesses and finally entry into the business with increasingly demanding tasks. Her father looks forward to his retirement and her succession.

A gap between intention and reality may have to be worked out, as happened in this fourth-generation family conglomerate:

The third generation learned from past history. Even though members of the third generation were sitting on the boards and ready to start making decisions, the second generation remained very much involved behind the scenes, second-guessing decisions officially made by the board. But now that the fourth generation is coming to power, the third-generation board members are stepping away from leadership— and not interfering with decision-making.

Diverse Pathways to Transition

The transition to professional management takes different forms in different cultures around the world.[10] Sometimes becoming a disciplined business means confronting traditional cultural values about business, family, and leadership. Here are several such examples.

Family 1: A third-generation family member from an Asian conglomerate observed how the influence of Confucian values adds additional complexity to the professionalization process. The strict confidentiality of the elder leaders coupled with the need to respect their rule kept the younger generation from making needed input. In this case, the patriarch is 90 while two highly educated and competent generations wait for their turns. In the meantime, necessary changes are delayed.

10 James Grubman and I have written about this in the book, **Cross Cultures: How Global Families Negotiate Change Across Generations** (Family Wealth Consulting, 2016). We present three cultural styles and show how family culture is influenced by each one as well as the results of family members being affected by their exposure to the other styles.

RESILIENCE OF 100-YEAR FAMILY ENTERPRISES

Family 2: In another Asian family, all three brothers worked in the business that was their father's dream. They worked collaboratively, but as the next generation grew up, the family decided that to remain connected, they wanted to have more fun together and engage in more non-business activities. To do so, they had to modify their traditional work ethic to be less restrictive and demanding.

Family 3: When the third generation came into power in another diversified business, they inherited assets that were conservatively managed by trustees. But they were more entrepreneurial and initiated a process of revision that took over 15 years. They added a holding company and board, with branch membership and active family governance by good professional managers.

Family 4: A nineteenth century patriarch passed ownership to his daughter. She immediately fired him and began to develop professional management. He was surprised and a little hurt but accepted her decision. As the third generation came to power, they wanted to remain unified and avoid conflict, so they created a 10-year voting trust. After a generation of professional management, a family CEO was selected from the next generation.

When the family was engaged early, several families reported that the next generation leadership team was prepared and ready to take over leadership when their time arrived. There was a clear timetable for the retirement of the older generation. Such anticipation and preparation is certainly not the norm in family enterprises, but in our generative family group, it happened more often than not in an orderly, predetermined path.

One family had a clear business challenge on their horizon. They saw the digital age coming and needed a visionary leader to help them navigate it. But at the same time, the family was satisfied with their distribution and was not willing to look for one. Their business didn't evolve, and they finally had to sell it. In another family, the fourth generation wanted to appoint a nephew as chair, while others felt he wasn't quite up to the job. The fourth generation appointed him, changed their mind, then selected another family member who is now chair. If they weren't deeply engaged with each other, this process would have dissolved in conflict.

Another family appointed an interim non-family CEO, to mentor the G5s. As described below, they then recruited a permanent, non-family CEO:

We want to maintain our values in how we approach people. I am confident now that this will happen with our new CEO. When he first came on three years ago, he didn't understand how important our values were. Now he sees that they are part of our DNA, and they have become part of his language and awareness.

Unexpected tragedy can strike at any time. In one business, a designated successor died in war. His younger brother reluctantly took over out of a sense of duty to the family. He was confident but unhappy. Nevertheless, he made things ready for the next generation and prepared for a transition to professional management. His successor was from outside the family.

Another family had a tradition of keeping a majority of independent directors on their board. After the unexpected death of the heir apparent, they looked for a new family leader. The best candidate was from a minority-owning family branch. Another family with a majority of independent directors on their board was negotiating a sale. When the sale fell through, they appointed a non-family CEO and asked him to professionalize the business. He had a private equity background and was expected to look for acquisitions and bring them to the family.

HOW OPPORTUNISTIC INNOVATION, BUSINESS DISCIPLINE, AND A CULTURE OF STEWARDSHIP GUIDE THE JOURNEY ACROSS GENERATIONS

Several families in our study initially handled succession by seniority. In one business, a brother ran things for a while, then his brother took over for the next for ten years. Models like this often break down due to unexpected events or difficulties with the next candidate in line. Other families sustain a long term, two-generation partnership; this allows the new leader to develop over time.

Family members can face conflicts of interest between their branch of the family and the whole business. Ownership is often apportioned by branches; one branch may have more ownership or even a majority. In this situation, family members need to ask: "Am I acting in the best interests of my branch or the whole business?" As an example, one third generation group observed a jockeying for succession in their parents' generation. They confronted them directly and said, *"We know you are not comfortable, but you need to trust us to be fair and not interfere."* The third generation then recruited a non-family leader. Yet another path is to have each sibling lead his or her own business while a holding company oversees their results and keeps them accountable.

Troubled Transitions

The examples discussed above were successful transitions. Other families were not so lucky. Several families appointed seemingly competent and experienced non-family CEOs who ultimately did not fit the family culture. One CEO who was used to having his own power and authority could not work with the family owners or the key executives. He was eventually forced out. Different variations of this scenario have taken place in other families in transition. One family proudly proclaimed that the third candidate that held the job was finally a fit.

A non-family CEO in a family business has a different role than a CEO of a public company; he or she must introduce significant business changes while respecting the culture and long-standing traditions of the family owners.

Another family appointed a non-family CEO to turn around their deteriorating business. He was successful in turning the business around, but the family had not installed family governance and oversight. This led to what they called a "power vacuum" in which the family was unable to make key ownership decisions. Because of this, the business was not able to innovate or move in new directions even though it was operationally successful.

In another family, a brother was asked to take the role of CEO. He was confident but ineffective, so the family asked him to step down. He was very upset at this and began to tell his son bad things about the family. Since then, there has been continual tension that the fourth-generation leaders have had to struggle to overcome.

Sometimes, the business outgrows family capability. Several families have a family and non-family CEO team working together; sometimes the roles are differentiated as family Chairman and non-family CEO. This can be a challenging but rewarding partnership if they are able to be open and candid while respecting each other's authority. Facing a large number of cousins in the next generation causes some families to decide to sell the company and cash out. Other families create financial partnerships allowing individuals more flexibility about their level of participation.

RESILIENCE OF 100-YEAR FAMILY ENTERPRISES

PROFESSIONALIZATION OF FAMILY LEADERS

Parallel to the support of non-family leadership, family members may also need to upgrade their own business knowledge and skills. As they grow up, members of each generation of a generative family have the option of working in one of the family enterprises and perhaps advancing to a leadership position. But as the business grows and the family's ventures become more complex, opportunity comes with conditions. The family now clearly defines the responsibilities of working in the family business. Family employees must be capable, open to collaboration with non-family employees, and have the accountability and discipline that befits a business professional.

When young family members become owners, they are not necessarily expected to become operational business leaders. By the third generation, if the family continues to own their legacy business, they usually transition from family operator/leaders to board and governance roles. They might also be employed but ascending to business leadership is not assured. In the new business culture, family members do not come first. Instead, the family extends its values about accountability, transparency, and long-term development to include non-family leaders as true partners. Professionalism and accountability within the family sends an important message to non-family leaders: You don't have to worry that family members will limit your promotion.

During school-age years, most families encourage internships or summer job programs that introduce family members to the family legacy. After these initial programs, family employment may diminish as young family members attend college and, often, graduate school. They may travel or perform some sort of service work as they pursue early stages of their career outside the family orbit. Most families have a policy of requiring younger members to work several years in another business before they can be considered for a position in the family business or family office. To reenter, a family member seeking a career has to exhibit professional business skills comparable to their non-family peers. In each succeeding generation, the desired or expected level of professionalism rises. By the fourth generation, emerging family leaders tend to seek roles in governance rather than operations.

When young family members seek an executive or leadership role, there is inquiry, assessment, and mutual dialogue about entry. By the third generation there may be many family and non-family candidates; at this point, favoritism for close family members can become an issue. To counter the tendency to promote their own children, the family makes the selection process explicit, transparent, and fair. When they apply for a job, family candidates usually must go through a parallel family vetting process, since, as potential owners, they have a privileged role and will be seen differently.

Several issues are considered in family vetting.

● First, the family must assess the capability and suitability of the candidate for the position.

● Second, there needs be awareness of the effect on other employees of placing a family member in a role. What message will the employees take from this? Will they be concerned about the impact on their prospects for advancement?

● Third, there may be competition within the family; another family member may expect to be chosen for the position. Cases like these must be mediated lest the dispute spills over into the business.

HOW OPPORTUNISTIC INNOVATION, BUSINESS DISCIPLINE, AND A CULTURE OF STEWARDSHIP GUIDE THE JOURNEY ACROSS GENERATIONS

As a third-generation family leader noted, family involvement should be modulated to an appropriate level:

When I was growing up, the employees worried that there were too many family members working in the business. My generation wasn't really encouraged to work in the business, so this situation changed. Now we hear employees are concerned that the family doesn't have enough family members working in the business; they worry about the family's commitment. So, now, we're trying really hard to recruit family members to work in the business. It seems like things will flip again.

Another member reported on the need to create a fair balance of capability and opportunity:

We have employment policies about working in the family businesses. We say that you need to have the same entry qualifications as an outsider or better. There are two angles to that. My personal opinion is that if you become too prescriptive, it pushes family members away. They say it's too bureaucratic and it seems like you don't want us in the business. I think it has to be balanced.

To develop competent leadership, many families create a long-term leadership development plan. This can be very traditional. For example, a fifth-generation European manufacturing firm has established a clear process for succession. Co-CEOs are appointed each generation to represent the two owning branches. A daughter, who is in line to become the successor from her family branch, recounted how the process began with her appointment when she was in university and the years of preparation that she needed before she could take up her role. While this is a risky choice, the family benefits because it is predictable and makes the process clear to each member of the new generation.

Most of our families require family members to work outside before applying, as in this example:

We've had several fourth-generation family members hired over the last five to seven years who secured jobs appropriate to their skill sets after outside employment. In fact, we've only had one family member who didn't have outside experience, and this didn't go as well.

The message that attracts a family member to the business is important. Sometimes, a feeling of obligation brings him or her in. One leader notes that he was recruited to save the business. Because he was concerned about its decline and was an experienced businessman, he felt he had to intervene. The most talented family members clearly have other options. Often, they are entrepreneurs themselves and want to forge their own paths. Nevertheless, the family might call and make them an offer. A father called his son when he was 25 and asked if he was interested. The son noted that this call "planted a seed," and, a few years later, he was ready for the offer. He and his family moved from the city where he worked for a bank back to the small town he grew up in.

Some families want family employees to start at the bottom, but when this happens, most families fast-track young leaders up the ladder:

When I joined the business, I started on the shop floor, then went from manufacturing to sales, and then slowly, slowly, took a long time to get to where I am today. It was a long, very drawn out process. I'm sure they have some kind of a process in place today but not like what it used to be.

Generally, you don't need to work outside just to join the business. But I know a few who worked outside first. The company has something called the fast track to a higher position. So, you can work outside and then come in at a vice president level and advance further.

RESILIENCE OF 100-YEAR FAMILY ENTERPRISES

As his family enterprise was undergoing a major transformation from products to business services, a young family member saw an opportunity to make a major contribution to this effort. He was attracted to the challenge, not the opportunity for secure employment, but he demonstrated his capability from prior experience. As an engineer, he was eager to put his experience to work developing sustainable factory practices; this would be a new expectation for this company. He asked if he could develop a project where family initiative would implement sustainability in its manufacturing operations. As a young person, however, he quickly became aware how hard it was to develop credibility and get the employees to adopt his plan. Still, after a longer period than he had imagined, he completed the project. He was then promoted to manufacturing operations where he was able to work collaboratively with non-family executives who shared his values and commitment and respected his capability.

If a family encourages many family members to enter the business, as a minority of our families do, they set up mechanisms for evaluation, career guidance, and promotion to leadership designed specifically for family employees. Because of the number involved and the possibility of conflict about a sensitive issue, they develop clear policies about employment— policies that are clearly differentiated from governance roles. One large family has a "family relationship manager" whose job is to support and assess the competence of family members. Several families require family employees to undergo a special assessment as they approach leadership level.

Others have active programs in which a young family member is given a trusted non-family leader as a mentor. This builds bonds between family and non-family management and helps family members see that their authority and skill as a family member must defer to and respect the outside leadership. This collaboration and meritocracy is helpful when filling key posts as they become open. Will it be a family member or not? Increasingly, family members are given less preference.

In another situation, two family members wanted to rise in the business. This presented both a family and a business challenge:

> In the third generation a position came up, and a few family members applied. One of the family members that applied had worked in the business for about 20 years. Another person that applied hadn't worked in the business that long at all. He was just a college student who went away for his education. He got his outside grants, then came back and applied for this supplemental position. But this younger guy actually got the position instead of the one that had the experience. So that created an issue, both on a business level and a family level.

> I saw this firsthand because both individuals were in my branch of the family. It definitely damaged relationships. Things have gotten a lot better, but I know these two individuals will struggle with hard feelings for a long time. But the decision was made, and a lot of things went into it, and I personally feel it was the right decision. The right person got the position. In spite of this, you can see how the individual who had years of experience in the business would think, "I should be the most qualified" even though in reality he wasn't.

> One problem with this event was that too much personal information was shared with too many people. This was not professional. The leaders learned that personal things, especially about performance, shouldn't be shared so openly.

As the business culture shifts, family engagement by a generative family is not swept aside in favor of professional leadership. Rather, as accountability for business results increases, family members from the current and the rising generations realize that they must add to their level of professional skills in order to serve. The family initiates an active process to set standards and develop skills, commitment and value-adding roles for rising generation family members, who are new owners and owners-in-waiting. A previous working paper, **Releasing the Potential of the Rising Generation** (2015) documented the steps in this direction taken by such families.

Activities that develop "professional" family members include:

- Setting clear expectations for consideration of hiring by the business,

- Encouraging outside learning (university, business programs),

- Requiring candidates to work for X years for other businesses,

- Carefully crafting messages about family hiring for both family and non-family staff,

- Designating a "family relationship manager" to support family education and development,

- Making evaluation of family transparent and separate from filial lines,

- Keeping individual personnel decisions private and professional,

- Regularly communicating about how the system is working and willingness to make changes.

ENTREPRENEURIAL FOCUS FOR EACH NEW GENERATION

In order to succeed over several generations, generative families have discovered that it is not enough to just have a professional, disciplined family company. Growth and expansion of a legacy company cannot continue at a geometric pace, even though the family is growing geometrically. The family must find ways to be innovative and opportunistic. The craftsman path must be supplemented by opportunists.

A stale, predictable business, even if such a thing could survive today, does not greatly interest the most talented members of the next generation. These young people often have attractive outside options, so the family enterprise must compete for their attention. A disciplined professional business may be profitable, but not innovative or opportunistic. The challenge for every family is to develop the entrepreneurial mindset and requisite skills in key members of each generation. Here's a report from a fourth-generation business:

> One of the big challenges for a fourth-generation business, rare as they are, is how to keep the entrepreneurial spirit alive. We need to keep the business innovative and productive, and we have to create an entrepreneurial mindset in the governance of the business. The company has to make sure that the businesses are growing, entrepreneurial, creative, and innovative. I hope we have the right people in place to ensure that.

> There's a new dimension that we're beginning to play with. We ask, "If you're part of this family clan, what does it mean to you as an individual? You're wealthier than your neighbor, but is this enough or is there something else?" One European business family I admire a lot said, "Well, in fact, you have more opportunities to develop yourself as a person when you're part of such a clan. You also have a good chance to become outstanding in terms of entrepreneurship." I very much like this vision, and I'm trying to promote it.

RESILIENCE OF 100-YEAR FAMILY ENTERPRISES

Encouraging Entrepreneurship

While the business develops core competencies over generations, the rising generation frequently wants to see the family move into new areas. This fourth-generation family leader, in a business that started in farming and forest products, then expanded into newer areas like media and entertainment, observes:

> *We're trying to promote entrepreneurship among the young generation. I wish I could learn what interests them most about coming into the company. I wonder what's going on in the company that they don't want to be involved in, and what strategies they do want to pursue. We haven't been very successful at pulling this out of them, but they're young and it takes a lot of thought to come up with answers to those questions.*

> *Being in the venture capital business has been interesting for our family members because we've been opportunistic even if we don't have a well-defined group of industries or businesses we've been investing in. We take the view that we can identify technologies or businesses that are truly disruptive and have huge global sales potential provided we can understand enough about what the business is actually doing. Flexibility is what we're good at.*

> *We've been in commodity businesses, so we know how to judge different kinds of risk. Having a multitude of businesses really does limit risk. We stay away from popular trends. But if the focus of the opportunity is related to any process we know about like processing water or materials or anything that has to do with agriculture, then we take an interest. It turns out there's a pretty broad range of things we know a lot about, and we can apply the lessons we've learned to our new acquisitions. So, we're able to bring things to the party that make us an attractive investor. For instance, we've connected small companies with engineering expertise that would have taken them forever to find.*

A family wants the most talented and capable family members to be "in the business, not starting their own business on the outside," notes one fifth generation family leader. While preparing to retire, he was selecting the next generation of leadership for his family's holding company.

The entrepreneurial focus takes divergent, creative forms. It builds on long-term commitment, family values, and business discipline while adding elements of risk and seeking out new ventures. One family has two fourth-generation co-leaders. They recruited a team of non-family leaders and began acquiring new businesses, all within the framework of their family's values. Another very old European business expects each young person to go his or her own way, either operating one of their current businesses or starting their own under the family name. There are clear paths and support for family members to start new ventures and clear accountability for results.

Another European family business had a successful publicly-traded clothing company under the leadership of a third-generation family member. One of his cousins with a background in high tech asked to join the family business and be funded to set up new businesses. They were hugely successful. Eventually his branch separated from the other branch associated with the public clothing company.

HOW OPPORTUNISTIC INNOVATION, BUSINESS DISCIPLINE, AND A CULTURE OF STEWARDSHIP GUIDE THE JOURNEY ACROSS GENERATIONS

A question that often arises is whether entrepreneurship and new business is a continuation of the family enterprise or the start of a new enterprise, as it was in this Asian family:

> *The business leaders must learn to let go of their power and allow the next generation their own dreams and visions. They must be entrepreneurial enough to start up their own businesses and not just rely on the family enterprise.*

> *I will show my children that if they have the vision to build their own businesses, we will invest in their businesses, so we can move them to a different level. But my investment will not be majority ownership; I will be an angel investor. I would like my children to be entrepreneurs with their own passion and vision.*

> *When we do that, however, will it still the business founded by our ancestors? I would say that the wealth was given to the younger generation by the ancestors, but they created the new enterprises in the portfolio. In Asia, families have traditionally made money because of opportunity, not passion. But now, when the successors invest their money, they are passionate about changing the world. This is totally different from the way the business started. We have to give credit to these young entrepreneurs who have transformed the company and brought it into the modern world.*

Growth Versus Preservation

As each generation ascends, there is rarely unanimity in the dialogue between entrepreneurialism and conservatism. As we see in this next account, conflict between these competing views can tie up the business:

> *When our family started, our business was like a beautiful, exquisite, massive diamond. We took that diamond and put it in a safe. A couple of times a year, we take it out and look at it and then put it back. Now, a hundred years later, the same diamond sits in the safe. Nothing else has happened really. Now there are more people who want to take it out and look at it, but it can't survive long-term like that. I don't know if all of my generation feels the same way about it. Generation four has split into two camps over the issue of growth versus preservation. One camp says, "Let's just hold onto what we have." The other says, "Let's get creative and grow and make some money!" And because it's family and we have representative governance, nothing ever happens. We have to find a way to solve this conflict and move ahead.*

The older generation may want the enterprise to continue, but as they age, and the new generation matures, they may avoid or delay real change until they get the support of the rising generation. This report illustrates this dilemma:

> *We are now a holding company with print media, television, real estate, forestry, venture capital, and insurance. My dad and uncle postponed a lot of big decisions because we were not doing well in the '80s and they wondered if the family was going to be interested in continuing the business into the next generation. Now, because they postponed a lot of investment decisions, my generation has to decide whether to continue the business and how to set things in motion again.*

RESILIENCE OF 100-YEAR FAMILY ENTERPRISES

The Entrepreneurial Mindset

If a family has a talented and capable family team entering the third or fourth generation, they can create a family investment group. The group described below was organized by a family with two large unrelated legacy businesses and a passion for growth and entrepreneurship in their new generation:

> The way the G3 cousins take on new businesses evolved over the years. In the early stages of our career path, we didn't have a process, but everybody took an interest. Everybody wanted to look at new opportunities, so, we formed a company among the five of us. It was informal at first. We just got together and started saying, "Look, I found this business," or "I've got this idea." From there we started to grow a portfolio. Every year we allocate a certain amount of money to that investment portfolio. Now we have what we call the Family Bank. We do some research and find some promising stocks to buy. Then we bring them back to Dad, and he says, "This isn't the time to expand." But we just keep pushing and pushing until he finally comes around. These ideas have all come from our club; we bring the ideas and then we finance them.

Many generative families explicitly encourage family members to invest in new areas. A handful of families have experimented with a family bank or a family venture fund where family members can find funding for new ventures. For example, *"Our family bank allows members to find funding for projects they believe will bring either a financial return or a return in terms of human capital."*

In the following passage, a large global family enterprise—owning more than a hundred businesses— describes how they have institutionalized entrepreneurship in each generation:

> Each business operates as an independent unit with a board and a strategy committee composed of family and non-family members. We are an entrepreneurial family and we want to stay that way. We've encouraged younger members to prove themselves by setting up businesses. If younger members are passionate about something, we help them to set up a business around it. They can make mistakes without criticism or reprimands. Somebody might want to set up a business in IT, somebody else wants to start a theme park, and a third person wants to do a retail business. They're all encouraged to go ahead. This is an ongoing effort—and this is why we have so many businesses.

A fourth-generation family created a seven-member growth committee:

> We base membership on their careers and experience, not on their family branch. They get together a few times a year to discuss how to grow the business. It's a great idea in theory, but nothing seems to come from it. The members of this growth committee put a lot of time and effort into developing ideas and suggestions. Then, when they take them to the board of directors, the board supports them, but we don't see any results. Hopefully it will turn into something more than just talking about ideas.

There is not always a connection between the entrepreneurial mindset in the family and the entrepreneurialism of the business. In one large family business, non-family leaders were moving forward with many innovations. The family leader asked if they wanted to have the family review what they were doing. The leaders said it wasn't necessary, but the family leader said, "Are you willing to take all this risk, and be responsible if it doesn't work out, or do you want the family to sign off on it?" The business leaders then educated the family and got their informal buy-in and commitment.

HOW OPPORTUNISTIC INNOVATION, BUSINESS DISCIPLINE, AND A CULTURE OF STEWARDSHIP GUIDE THE JOURNEY ACROSS GENERATIONS

Another family leader observes:

> *Each generation of our family respects the business they've received from the generation above them, but then they begin to change it and grow it in their own way. Nobody comes into the business and assumes that he or she is just going to ride it out. Everybody comes with an idea of continual entrepreneurship and growth.*

Another family, entering its fourteenth generation as a business family, long ago moved from a legacy family business to many investments. They proudly note their focus on individual entrepreneurship while they continue to pool their investments as an extended family:

> *Our own children worked together for about 10 years in the same business. At that point, they decided to move on, and they all started their own businesses. They took a big portion of the money and put it into a common pool that they will look at in another five years. They've all invested in each other's companies, and they all sit in each other's boards. It's a strange way of continuing an enterprise, but in this family the entrepreneurial drive is too strong to focus on only one business. We view all of our children as G1 in the business, even though they're fourteenth generation from the standpoint of the family.*

To release opportunistic innovation, the family must link attitudes and encouragement with concrete actions. The clearest way a family does this is by setting aside family funds to support innovation, new ventures and various forms of social entrepreneurship by the rising generation of family members. As the call upon the family to reconsider the meaning of its values and apply them in practice, they ask the family to allocate funding and investments for such ventures. The family rightfully asks for accountability, but the active process of looking at new value-based ventures in generative families combines intention with clear pathways to action.

RESILIENCE OF 100-YEAR FAMILY ENTERPRISES

STORY #3: A YOUNG ENTREPRENEUR BUILDS
A NEW BUSINESS WHILE IN COLLEGE

In 1972, I was 18, and the Vietnam War was just ending. A lot of things were moving to the Pacific because there was a huge military presence there. I noticed a Chinese King Fu picture was doing very, very well in the theatre. I remembered during my schooldays in Hong Kong, once or twice a year my dad would bring back some free tickets for a movie. He would tell us how he invested some money with a few of his friends in producing this film.

I wrote to my dad: "Chinese karate pictures are doing well. Can you send me some of those from home? Maybe I can make some money on them." So, he sent me some posters, and I knocked on the door of the local theatre and asked for an appointment with the manager. I showed him the posters and said, "These are great movies; can we do some business?" He says, "Yeah, bring the movies in and we'll play them in the theatre. If one of them grosses more than $15,000, you'll get 35%. If it's less than that, you'll get 25% of the gross box office." I sent him the movies, they played them, and in a week, I think it grossed over $20,000. I got $7,000. The owner of the film told my dad, "Tell your son whatever revenue he can get, he'll keep 50% and give 50% back to the company."

So, as a college student, I made $3,500 in one week. That was a huge amount of money then. At that time, it cost just $1,800 to buy a car, So I started to grow that business with a few films my dad's friends had, and then came to Hong Kong to buy more. We took them to the Pacific Islands. We built a little big business by the time I graduated from college.

Taking Action In Your Own Family Enterprise

Culture Assessment

The foundation for the generative alliance is developing a culture that expresses the long-term goals, values, and intentions of the family owners. This section has described each element of successful long-term family enterprise culture.

After reading the stories in this section, you might take the opportunity to assess your own family enterprise culture. Considering the six elements we described, apply them to the culture and practices in your own family enterprise. You can use the table below as a template to conduct your assessment.

For each element consider:

● To what degree have you have implemented this?

● What do you do in this area that strengthens your family enterprise?

● What challenges or warning signs of strain are you facing in this area?

● What future steps might you take to develop this further?

ELEMENT	DEGREE USED (LO/MED/HI)	STRENGTHS FOR YOU	CHALLENGES FOR YOU	FUTURE STEPS
Long-Term Commitment				
Desciplined Professional Business				
Extend Family Values To Business				
Collaboration With Non-Family Leadership				
Professional Family Leadership				
Entrepreneurship In New Generations				

Implementing Culture Change

Obviously, these are very subjective and systemic issues, and it makes very little sense to fill this out alone. The best way to work on this sort of assessment is by naming a family Task Force. This can consist of the family leaders or a representative group of family owners and engaged members. Or, it might be made up of a cross-generational group that also contains some non-family leaders. The point is not just to complete the task but to open up each area of culture for discussion. The discussion should lead to some sort of Action Plan in which the leadership looks to further develop the openness, adaptability, accountability, and innovative spirit of all the family enterprises.

RESILIENCE OF 100-YEAR FAMILY ENTERPRISES

Part Five – Becoming Active Owners and Stewards: Guidance with an Engaged, Professional Board

A family business begins with a visionary founder/owner/operator. The subsequent generation often continues to view ownership as connected with operations. However, as the legacy business is harvested, and a third generation comes of age, they usually discover that ownership is very different from operations. The owners have to make decisions about the fate of the business and balance the use of resources, and to reach out to non-family executives and advisors. They also have to decide how to use their wealth: should it be reinvested, used for the benefit of the family, or employed for other purposes like philanthropy? As owners, their focus shifts from operating a business to overseeing family and non-family leaders and making choices about resources.

For at most two generations, a family enterprise can run on an ad hoc basis with little defined structure. But danger lies ahead. At some point, the business will become too complex to manage ad hoc, and conflicts may emerge among family members. One third-generation family member notes that, *"the key problem was lack of clarity in the organization about basic goals and mission and in understanding who decides these things. There were no job descriptions and no contracts for family members working in the business, so everything was kind of up in the air."*

The transition from family business to business family is more than a change in how the company is managed. Family members must submit to the discipline of a professional business and play the role of responsible owners. They can't use the business as a personal bank or employment resource. Even if there is a single family leader, the family has to move beyond being taken care of by this leader and take active responsibility for overseeing the new structure.

To create, sustain, and adapt the family culture and values over generations, the family must be aligned, make fast and effective business decisions, and implement them. Shared cultural values, policies, and practices do not just emerge. The family has to sustain them by resolving differences and making painful choices. There is often family upheaval as owner/managers must change their behavior and become more accountable. The process by which the family owners collectively organize themselves to develop resilience in dealing with internal family affairs and external business challenges is **governance.** Through each successive generation, generative families evolve active and complex systems of governance. They listen to many voices and resources and translate what they learn into effective operations, clear decisions and adaptive responses to new challenges.

Family enterprise governance is the structure by which disparate elements of the generative family alliance become aligned and integrated in practice. They need to listen to and balance the voices and perspectives of each group of stakeholders: family owners, young family owners-to-be, married-in spouses, key family executives, and advisors. Different views are raised and balanced within the family ownership group and the board. Out of this, decisions are made that serve the multiple purposes and constituencies of the family.

Our previous working paper described **family governance** as the emergence of activities, working groups, and policies that enable the family to realize its dreams and values in personal relationships and non-business activities.[11] This final section outlines how business governance listens and acts on these different concerns to create a generative family and its business enterprises.

Rising generations may not easily understand the difference between management and ownership. First and second generations are often hands-on business owner/operators. They tend to see ownership as holding title to a property, not as a complex structure that oversees business operations. But as more family members grow up who do not expect to be operators, the ownership role becomes increasingly important. As the third and fourth generations come of age, they become more aware of the tasks and functions of their role as owners. Family members want to know how exactly they can make appropriate decisions about their business while delegating operations to non-family leaders.

Because owners have ultimate control over family ventures, they must exercise this control actively and responsibly. They have to stay informed, make tough choices, and make sure they are implemented. Even when they appoint a board, there are still areas where family owners must decide and act. The board asks the owners to tell them the general direction they want for the business, how much risk and reinvestment there will be, and what values the enterprise will be based upon. As each generation includes new owners, they will return to these questions at regular intervals. Agreements that limit voting control to those with special classes of stock or to trustees must be taken into account. But, because this is a family, the formal owners usually want to listen to views and concerns beyond a narrow leadership circle.

The third generation usually contains more family owners than can sit comfortably together around a table. Hence, they must organize some form of representative group to manage their interests. They can't all exercise direct ownership effectively. Because young family members are continually coming of age, the elder owners want to listen to those who will eventually become owners. To sustain a vibrant portfolio of business and financial activities, the multi-generational family develops business governance mechanisms containing oversight entities. **This "board of directors" is a creation of the owners and usually includes both family members and independent, non-family members who are not owners. The board oversees, sustains and develops the family enterprise for the growing number of owners.**

BEYOND SELF-INTEREST: BECOMING STEWARDS

What does it mean to be an owner of a family enterprise? The family goes through a learning process to develop this complex role. Responsible family owners must have the capability to oversee businesses and investments that may have grown to huge proportions; to accomplish this, they will need to draw upon non-family resources.

Every family enterprise must consider the kind of owners they want to be. As we have shown, a generative family chooses ownership that is actively engaged in the values and culture of their family enterprises. They act as **stewards,** producing wealth that has lasting and appreciating value with an eye toward providing for generations to come. Unlike other types of owners, they are concerned about more than their individual self-interest. Together, owners share values and are aligned about what they want and where they are going.

11 Our previous working paper, **Governing the Family Enterprise: The Evolution of Family Councils, Assemblies and Constitutions** (2017), deals with the "business of the family" and, therefore, has some overlap with this section. It outlines how governance evolves, and how governance diverges into strains of family and business governance. The section on Owners' Councils especially connects to the material in this section.

RESILIENCE OF 100-YEAR FAMILY ENTERPRISES

As owner/stewards, they are active, thoughtful, vigilant, and resilient in how they exercise their care for the family enterprises. Stewardship is difficult to mandate; it is a complex conception of responsibility that is part of the culture of the family enterprise. It is learned, absorbed, accepted, and internalized by the whole extended family.

While ownership can be dispersed among many family members, the enterprising family wants to assure that control over major decisions is in the hands of family members who protect and look after **all** family members, not just the most prominent current owners. As a group of owners, they differentiate their own self-interest from that of the family as a whole. Many family enterprises fail because individual needs are not subjugated to the family as a whole. The concept of **stewardship** arises when an owner shifts from maintaining a personal agenda to considering the best interests of all the family stakeholders. He or she may even go beyond the family, adding concerns for non-family leaders, employees, and others in the community. Stewardship is a form of self-interested altruism.

Active owners/stewards answer to several non-owner stakeholder constituencies:

- Other family members, especially the rising generations of young family members.

- Employees, suppliers, and customers who can be deeply connected to the family.

- Community members who are affected by them and who influence their actions.

A steward is more than a fiduciary who looks out for the best interests of the individual business. Stewards feel a responsibility to future owners and others who are influenced by and connected to the enterprise. A steward has a broader focus than a passive, less involved owner. This focus leads them to be concerned about conflicts between short and long-term goals and disagreements among different stakeholder groups.

The extended family is part of a family "tribe" with shared values and personal relationships. Therefore, when the board (and/or the owners and trustees) make business decisions, they feel a responsibility to be attuned to the views of constituents who may not be owners. This sense of responsibility differs significantly from the approach of a board in a non-family business, where responsibility is narrower.

To attend to the opinions, concerns, and needs of all the family shareholders, generative families convene multiple family or owners' groups who advise and raise issues to the family leaders (we will expand on this in a later section). Generative families then operate as a unified owners group with a long-term vision and perspective. As they develop an engaged board of directors with significant input from independent, non-family, directors, the stewardship orientation is expressed through governance and the oversight of family enterprises.

THE RISE OF GOVERNANCE

When a next generation leader transforms the business into a disciplined, professional entity, the rest of the family may feel sidelined, even though they usually enjoy the financial benefits. The challenge comes when there isn't a clear successor and the family faces a major transition:

> *In the years my [third generation] father was CEO, a lot of wonderful things were accomplished. Before this, our ad hoc governance process had some holes, limits, and tensions arising as changes took place, so, in the late 90s, we decided to reorganize governance. When my father took over the company, he needed to get the business in shape, so he focused on strengthening the company and making it more productive.*

> *By the end of the '90s, he realized he had strengthened the company and made some pretty major changes. We went from a corporation to a limited partnership, but these changes made some members feel alienated. He realized he needed to strengthen the family ties to the business. That's when he helped start our family council.*

Conflict Around New Governance

Conflict can erupt when transforming a culture as family members lose status and roles. One member had the role of Shareholder Relations Manager; her task was to oversee the involvement of family members in the business. As she reports:

> *My position was created to work with the family. Some family members were asked to leave the business with the expectation that they would go outside, gain experience and then return. Some did, but some did not. A few older generation senior leaders were asked to leave or placed in different positions. Several family members were taken off the board and offered a slot on the owners' advisory council. That softened the blow, but at the end of the day, it was still really hard. But, because profits rose to new highs, the increased stock dividends made those wounds heal quicker.*

> *The **Owners' Advisory Council** represents all the family owners. Their vision is to promote harmony among the shareholder families and to enable them to speak with one voice. They set business goals, financial metrics, and risk management stewardship projects; then they work with the board to come to agreements on them. We don't want the owners' group to set hopes and expectations by talking to management—that's not their role. It's the board's job to hold management accountable, not the family. The other mission of the owner's advisory council is to help select and vote for board members.*

When a family enterprise "professionalizes," it recruits experienced outside advisors, independent directors, trustees, and non-family executives. The family respects them and their expertise and draws upon it to their benefit. However, because of the competence and firepower of these advisors, the family might step back and lose involvement with the business. As we see in this report, this can set up a cycle of family passivity and lack of development:

> *We have an outside advisor who is very, very—I'd say overly—involved. This is a real challenge for us. What should we do as a family and what should we look for from outside people? The more somebody from the outside does it, the less the family has to do, and this sets up a negative cycle. I'd really like to see our family take more initiative to do the things that we're paying someone else to do. It makes me very uncomfortable.*

RESILIENCE OF 100-YEAR FAMILY ENTERPRISES

Deepening the skills of craftsmanship with disciplined, professional business practices entails a corresponding shift of roles and awareness by family members. This process requires high involvement from both the family and the business board as each learns new roles and interactions. A member of a South American fourth generation family describes it this way:

> We're a very hands-on family, and we've transitioned into being a professional family business. But how do we engage with professionals? How do we let the CEO do his job while letting the board do their job? Since we separated our board from the family council, we sometimes step on each other's toes because the family council is used to acting as the board and being involved in everything. We've had to retrain ourselves to step back and be engaged but not interfere with the boards and our new CEO.

> We now face the challenge of buying a new core business and how we can, as cousins, work on that project together. The other challenge is that we have cousins who expect higher remuneration from their work in the business. How are we going to handle that, because we definitely want family members engaged? We want to be responsible shareholders and to be engaged in the business. But to be engaged, you have to know the business and to know the business, you have to participate somehow. The younger members especially need the hands-on experience. But, if there is a position, how do we match the job with their skill set? And how much are we going to pay them? This shift to a more professional business has become a huge challenge.

As stewards, active owners shift their mindset from protecting their own interests to looking ahead to everyone's best interest. This can be a challenge as this account illustrates:

> We needed to start thinking as one family instead of five branches. When you have several enterprises and a few foundations, you think, "I worry about my branch, I worry about my family and I want what is best for them." Every family does that. But to throw that out the window and say that we believe that a one-family approach is the right thing to do is a major challenge. Yes, we understand that this is going to happen at the fourth generation anyway, but we're doing it at the second-generation level. It's hard to develop that kind of trust with my brother and sister and say, "I may not have the ability to put my kids in a position of authority, but I can trust that you are going to have your kids in a position of authority to speak for all of us—to speak on behalf of the family." I think that was probably the biggest leap of trust. But in the end, we understood that we had to go through this and that it was a very difficult process. We struggled with it.

A trust structure with a trustee in charge can also cause family beneficiaries to feel disconnected and disenfranchised from the business. As a consequence, they may disengage and become passive spectators rather than active stewards. If this disengagement begins to take root, it must be reversed. Here is a family that took steps to engage family members within such a structure with positive results:

> I joined the Young Presidents Organization. In my first meeting, I described how we held stock in trust and that I'm the managing trustee. So, I control the company. But one of my friends said, "You're in big trouble. You don't have shareholders, you have coupon clippers and they're not paying any attention to what you're doing." That woke me up. We decided that the best shareholders are *educated* shareholders, so we launched a yearly family reunion and whole day business meeting to engage everybody, rekindle enthusiasm, and generate a sense of ownership. It's been extremely positive for the entire family to have this glue. We get great questions and reengagement and we return the next year and start all over. As a result, we're starting to get more continuity.

Complex Governance Structures

There can be a board for each entity, and sometimes boards report to other boards. This fifth-generation company has a unique two-board structure:

> For the last 20 years, we have operated in a dual board structure. Some may call it a family council, but there is actually a **corporate board of directors** with some family members and some non-family members that handles the week-to-week business. The philosophy and direction of the company is handled by what we call **the family board of directors.** Some might call this a family council, but we operate differently than a family council. We make motions and pass them; we act in a somewhat more official capacity than a family council. We all grew up in a very businesslike atmosphere, so that works best for us. The openness of both of those boards allows family members a certain "internship" for lack of a better term. Any family member over the age of 21 can commit to being on either of these two boards for a couple of years.

> My mother is 84 and has pretty much already turned business operations over to our family board. It still operates under her philosophy, but we're running the show. There are two things that our family is trying to reinforce now that we're through our generational change: expectations and the quantity of time spent together. Sometimes that time is filled with conflict and argument and even some pain, but the only way we get through that is by working through it together.

> The family board provides guidelines and criteria for the corporate board. This includes things like where we look for properties, final decisions on forming trusts, donations to the foundation, how many money managers we'd like to see—everything down to monthly decisions. That's why I say our family board of directors is not really a family council. It makes actual decisions; for instance, we tell the president of the company, "This is the direction we're moving in. We need you to help us get there."

By the fourth generation, the ownership group can be quite large. For example, one non-US family conglomerate began to ask how to stay connected with over 200 family owners. They created four governance boards to manage the complex relationships:

- An operating business;

- A family office (a subsidiary of the operating business);

- A foundation, a charitable arm of the family; and

- A family council, formed in 2004.

A family with a public and private company had boards for each one:

> The responsibility of the family council is high level oversight. They suggest potential new board directors in a prescribed process. We want the most qualified people serving in those positions. First, because it's a very large enterprise and, second, because it's a public company, and we want to make sure we are operating in the best way and have the best people making the key decisions.

> The second part of that oversight is the parallel planning. Parallel planning considers the concerns and desires of the families as majority shareholders and presents these to their board. The board is made up of primarily independent board members with family members as chair and vice chair. We present to

the board where we see growth, risk, liquidity, profitability, and what we are comfortable with. They review that and tell us, "The strategic plan we are working with addresses every one of those things." Alternately, they might say, "Our plan does not address liquidity. What should we be doing to look at that?" Or, they might ask, "Do the goals you are looking at make business sense?" As we discuss these things, the six family members out of the 18 on the board (plus the chair and vice chair who are family members) represent the families' parallel planning process. At the same time, we have a majority of independent directors and a non-family CEO, all of whom are trying to come up with what is best for the company and for the rest of the shareholders as well.

A previous working paper described the "two pillars" of governance: organization of the family through a family council, and of the business by a board of directors[12]. These two pillars—family council and board—are highly interconnected when it comes to overseeing the family enterprise. Here are governance documents from one family that define this interconnection and boundary:

*We have a shareholder agreement that lasts 10 years, and then we update or renew it. Company by-laws guide the business. The first document the family council developed was a **Family Charter**. It talks about what we're committed to—our core values and purpose as a family.*

The family charter sets the direction for the family within the family council. One of the big distinctions it makes is between the "business of the family," as opposed to the "business of the business." If we ever have to ask at a meeting if a topic is something we should be talking about or just the business of the business, somebody will say, "Wait a minute. I think we're almost crossing the line here." We can always get clarification if we need it.

*We've also developed an **Owner's Plan**, a document the family council generates and presents to the board each year. This plan gives direction about the interests of the family with regard to the business. We've found this to be quite useful, and the board has acknowledged that they find it useful to get the family's input on the direction of the company. The plan includes things like the level of risk we're comfortable with. And if, for example, the family says it's comfortable with "moderate risk", the plan even defines what we mean by moderate risk. This owner's plan hasn't changed much year to year, but we tweak it a little to get clarification based on the feedback and questions from the board. We've found this to be a valuable document for both sides.*

12 See **Governing the Family Enterprise.**

HOW OPPORTUNISTIC INNOVATION, BUSINESS DISCIPLINE, AND A CULTURE OF STEWARDSHIP GUIDE THE JOURNEY ACROSS GENERATIONS

STORY #4: OVERCOMING RESISTANCE TO GOVERNANCE

Governance can originate from any quarter: the next generation, the family, or the board. Its introduction often disturbs the equilibrium of the family/business entity because it entails limiting and regulating roles and distributing authority. Therefore, there is usually resistance. Here is how a fourth-generation family struggled to develop active family governance alongside their business board:

I joined the board 15 years ago. At that time, we hired a non-family CEO from another family company and he told us, "You guys need a family governance system." He announced this to the foundation board because it was the only place where the family members convened. I took on the task because I was interested. Nobody knew what family governance was or what it meant. We didn't necessarily have problems at that time, but this new CEO said, "You're a family business; you need family governance.

I initially encountered resistance at the board level because nobody understood what governance meant and didn't see the need for it. Later, when they heard that family governance involved creating a "family council," they got concerned that this council would become a "shadow board" and interfere with the operating company board. I was really worried about what this resistance meant for our family. Nevertheless, we began the process of gathering family members together, creating a family directory, and getting people to come to our first family meeting. The challenges along the way were huge because the board didn't understand what we were doing. Instead, they saw me as an agitator, akin to a union organizer, organizing the masses! They thought that the whole thing was a really bad idea. Their view was, run the business well, keep the shareholders at arm's length, and everything will be fine. The less we hear from them, the better.

It was a long, long process to create a family council. We first had to convince the board that we weren't going to interfere with the running of the business. We even listed the ways in which we were trying to provide a service to them. We told them that the family council would serve them by:

● Fostering a community that is connected and engaged, respects individual perspectives, and works together on shared goals;

● Facilitating communication within the family and between family and company;

● Representing the family in working with the board and management on projects of common interest;

● Nurturing strong and effective leadership;

● Promoting and providing continuing education among the family, board, and management;

● Upholding our family's values without continually having to prove ourselves to the board or to the family (who didn't really understand what we were doing either).

The family liked the idea of having a voice because that's the way we pitched it. But they were still skeptical, because they didn't really understand why they had to do anything. They had never had any sense of responsibility as owners. All they were doing was receiving dividends. It was a big challenge to gain legitimacy and credibility with the board and the family. We tried our best to lead them to the realization that, "Oh my God, we are owners of this company. That's a big responsibility, and there are certain things that I need to do to be prepared to be a good owner."

The sixth generation now understands this. They've been coming to the meetings, and that's been the theme over and over and over. They understand that involvement is necessary in a family business; it's become part of their DNA. The fifth generation keeps feeling a need to beat people over the head to justify our existence, but the sixth generation, especially the ones on the board, say, "Why are you doing this? It's not necessary. We get it. We get what you're doing." Now it's just a matter of how we move forward.

STORY #5: CLARIFYING STRUCTURE AND OWNERSHIP WHEN BECOMING A PUBLIC COMPANY

When a family business goes public, or when ownership is placed in a trust, the new status often means that previous family perks and practices can no longer continue. The family has to understand why this is necessary and learn other ways to balance personal and business needs. The owner's role radically shifts with the form of the business as this story illustrates:

From 2004 onward, the family council started evolving toward the trust structure. In the past, my grandfather simply decided how to use the money through an informal system of family benefits he provided to his children. Back then, it was just his children; the grandchildren, like myself, were very young. When we went public in 2004, we had to clarify the share structure. When your company is not listed, management can mingle personal and company money, but the listing process required us to clean up the share ownership process and the trust.

Two days from now, we're going to sign the family agreement that governs the relationship between my father and his trust and the rest of the family. My parents still control 35 percent of these shares, but the remaining 65 percent are in a trust to benefit future generations and provide liquidity for every branch of the family. The 35% funds the family office and will be used for family benefits and philanthropy. It also provides a single voting block for business decisions. The trustee, my father, has 35% voting rights. He named me successor trustee, so I will have to manage family involvement in the future. I will have control not only of my own shares but also the voting rights of the trust.

Another distribution goes to family owners whether or not they work in the business. Family members that work in the business get a market rate salary and bonus. The trustee balances family and business needs. Our challenge will come 30 years in the future when more family members may demand a high dividend.

Our investment committee meets quarterly, more often when there is an investment decision. I told my dad after the signing, "Dad, you cannot be in control of all these decisions. You must allow for a democratic process and let me manage the business with my brothers." We presented the case for major investment decisions and a secret ballot to approve them. We stated that the minority must respect the majority, and that vetoing should be done very, very seldom. We told him, "You must allow this process to happen because you won't be around forever. It's best that we start to work on this now while you're still here."

TRANSPARENCY AND THE VOICE OF THE FAMILY

Because a family is connected and shares values and concerns, the family needs to share information and be **transparent.** To respect shareholders and develop a generative alliance, a family enterprise must become an open and transparent body. This is particularly important as the older generation prepares the rising generation for leadership. Openness is also critical for family owners to make effective decisions that they can stand by. In the paternalistic view of many founders, informing family members is often low priority. Even the second-generation may not discuss business issues with the non-owning family members. Instead, family owners may be kept in the dark by elders as this family member reports:

> I went once a year to an event there, but I was sometimes ashamed because I knew so little about it. Dad didn't really tell much, and we didn't really ask. We didn't discuss how the family and the business intermingled until recently.

By the third generation the family begins to learn the importance of sharing business information within the family beyond the circle of major owners:

> Transparency obviously has been a huge push for us even in our business meetings. We start with just us—none of our executives—and we talk about our vision for the company, where we're going in the next year, what things we think are important about last year's performance and plans for the future. We field a few questions from the audience; then go through the financials with our CFO. Next, the auditor comes in and they get to ask him questions. Finally, the executives come in and present plans for each division.

Generative families create policies and activities that actively include family shareholders in governance, even if they have no formal authority or just a small ownership stake, as this family illustrates:

> Every six months, we have a shareholders' meeting in which all family members from age 16 and above learn about the financial performance of the business. We present the key strategic issues in each area of the business. We start with the vision and values, and we keep reinforcing them. Each time a new young member enters, we stress them vigorously to inculcate in them where we're coming from and where we've been.

> We have a family council, ownership council, and advisory board. The ownership council comprises those members of the family who have been working within the business; most of them evolved from the former business 18 years ago. The ownership council ensures that the advisory board oversees the appointment of the CEO and gauges his or her performance. The ownership council also oversees the bigger picture; deciding on the direction of the business is part of their role. The ownership council created the family constitution and periodically reviews and modifies it. For a while, it met quarterly; now it's every six months.

While the family owners and their designated board control the business, generative families are unique because they also take pains to communicate with all family members. They are prepared to listen to concerns and ideas from all parts of the family including non-owning family members and those whose ownership is in trust. Feedback from the family helps the owners to become aware of significant disagreements. For example, there might be disagreements about important matters like the sale of the business, major new investments, or new directions for the company. Listening to feedback can also make them aware of new ideas and opportunities. This transparency is important because new generation family members—the

RESILIENCE OF 100-YEAR FAMILY ENTERPRISES

children of these non-owners—may eventually become owners. The family realizes that informing them about the business and including them in discussions is critical for responsible future ownership. But this transparency and listening must also include the understanding that their input is strictly advisory and that the business leaders must make their own decisions.

Small family shareholders may not be fully informed about the business. Since all family members can't serve on the board, the family must develop opportunities to communicate with the board, learn about their decisions, and have a voice within those decisions. Here's how one family accomplished this:

> During our annual family meeting, we have one day in which the managers spend eight hours with the family talking about what's going on with the business. Then we do a half-day roundtable with the CEO and whoever he brings with him. Five or six people from management give talks to the family. That's a much smaller group, so you get a better sense of what the family is thinking about and what the business is doing. As the family chair of the board, I personally do presentations. This year, we are also going to all the sites around the world to talk about what the family is doing in terms of the transition. They know that the non-family CEO is reaching retirement, so we want to make sure that we close the circle in terms of communication.

> We have a family information meeting and lunch every second Tuesday. We get all family members working within the business to join us for an update on what's going on. The things we discuss may not all be business related; the purpose is just to keep the family working together, involved together, and knowing each other.

> It's critical to our success that communication channels with family members remain transparent in both directions; that's the only way to ensure that there's trust and harmony and support from the family. The day that trust breaks down is the day we'll lose the support of family members. Things will start falling apart if this becomes a widespread failing.

> The next generation voiced their concern for a more explicit system. It's been a learning process for everyone. I got involved very young because my parents told me that you're in a better position to participate than us, so go ahead.

> The family has a high level of integrity about our planning and structure governance. Those who choose not to be actively involved in the family can get information about why the family money is being handled in a certain way or why we're involved in certain businesses. We always try our very best to have individuals at the top of the industry involved alongside us; these include outside board members and directors.

> Generation five members said that they wanted to be more involved but acknowledged that they never opened the board packets. So, a number of years ago, we went electronic with our board packages so everyone in generations four and five gets a copy of a packet before every meeting. These packets include budgets, financials, investment portfolios, the minutes from every committee meeting, and all the ranch management board issues they are drafting. Many family members that aren't on the board don't open the board packets, but each person has to acknowledge that the information is there and decide how are they going to use it.

HOW OPPORTUNISTIC INNOVATION, BUSINESS DISCIPLINE, AND A CULTURE OF STEWARDSHIP GUIDE THE JOURNEY ACROSS GENERATIONS

When we started, there was zero visibility on the value of the business—no transparency or actual figures to review in terms of margin, or five-year plans. We would just have a very short presentation of general figures and dividends and that was it. Then some family shareholders started to ask questions about the management and the structure of the company. My family Group A has been much more directly involved than family Group B. So shareholders in Group B started asking, "Why aren't you more transparent to shareholders?"

A sixth-generation family with several hundred family shareholders operated with high transparency and inclusiveness. But the whole family together was too large an entity to decide business policy directly, so they created a full-time role of Family President. His or her role was to organize the business so that the family could give responsible and thoughtful input. How this occurred is described below:

In terms of the board of the company, there is always a preference given to family members. They make up the majority of the board, but over the years we've also welcomed non-family board members. We hired our first non-family CEO 12 years ago, and he's worked out extremely well. At that time—around 2001—my position as family president was created. People didn't know the new CEO very well and weren't confident that he could handle both the business and the family side of things. Every CEO before that had been a family member and wore both hats. At this time, however, we decided to split the position into a two-leader system of governance: CEO and family president.

Having a family president then gave rise to the idea of a family council. The family president is essentially the chairman of the family council. Before that we had a human resource committee of family members who would advise the family member president on family matters. Now, with the family council, we have a more formal arrangement for discussing family issues. One responsibility of the family president and the family council is to maintain the interest of the family in the business.

I sit on the board of directors. My job, along with the other family directors, is to make sure that business decisions track with family values. I'm asked, "How would the family feel about this?" Then I go back to the family council and use it as a sounding board to test ideas in the family. I also run family programs, including the big annual meeting. I have some staff allocated, and a family council committee helps plan it. This is a big part of our job because it's a huge meeting, and it's always pretty complicated.

There are now more places for family members to be involved. Someday we might have a new family member step up and be our CEO. Our nominating committee is unique. It's not a nominating committee for the board, but a hybrid of board members, family members, and family council members. Board members from the family are elected by this hybrid council as are associate directors. The nominating committee nominates the family president, the board endorses the nomination, and the family votes on that position.

We have the same problems that everybody does: people apply and if you don't give them the position, they're not happy. When it comes to the family council, we're usually looking for a certain talent. We try to hone in on that in the job description so that when people apply they get that we're looking, for example, for a younger person with social media skills. I think all nominating committees struggle with how people feel when they're rejected; we certainly don't have that one figured out.

We're trying to be conscious of the future through a strategic long-range planning exercise we do every ten years. We try to look at what lies ahead so that the new leaders of the business and the family will be ready and committed to both.

RESILIENCE OF 100-YEAR FAMILY ENTERPRISES

STORY #6: INTERPLAY OF FAMILY AND GOVERNANCE

The board and the family council each play a role in overseeing the family enterprise. The dividing line between the two is a moving target that must be set and maintained not by fiat, but by negotiation. The family initiates a cycle of advising and deciding, but then they defer to the board. The board listens to the family and then makes the difficult choices and explains them to everyone. Here is an account of how a manufacturing business entering its fourth generation deals with this interplay:

We're trying to come up with criteria for family board members. I've been on a number of other boards, so I know something about how boards work. We're also developing criteria for replacing the four family board members. None of us are planning to go anywhere soon, but we need to decide the criteria so that the fifth generation will know where to look if they want to be involved. They can learn what it means to be a board member. When I entered the board, I had no idea what I was getting into.

At every board meeting we have a summary report from the chair of the family council. At the family council, we have reports about the board meeting. They're usually back-to-back: the board meeting happens one day and then the family council meets the next day. In addition, we have a family relations subcommittee. This developed because our board chair wanted us to review our values. So I began with a review and an updating of current family values.

Q. Given the inclusive culture and complexity of your family, how do you take ideas from the family owners and distill them down to contribute to the business?

It has to do with role definition. For example, the family council does several key things. They develop the values that the whole company lives by, elect board members, and build family relationships that encourage stewardship. So that's the family council. The family assembly is held every other year, and anybody can volunteer to help out with that. We encourage stewardship and involvement, so a lot of people want to participate.

Recently we had a big project that focused on the salaries for family board members. The family council got involved in trying to analyze the salaries of the board members in general. However, that was just not appropriate; they didn't have the experience. So, the board chair took that back and said, "These kinds of decisions actually need to get made at the board level." We have to maintain those role definitions.

Q. Has there been a major family crisis, a transition or difficulty that has inspired better practices or different ways to work as a family?

When I got on the board, the whole selection and election taskforce was in major crisis. There was a lot of screaming by family members about this. We needed to develop our credibility with management as a family. We had gone through two CEOs in four years. When I came on board, I could see that the current CEO was not good for the company. This led to a big split in the family, though eventually everybody agreed with my assessment, and he transitioned out. The next CEO did some good things but was also not in line with the values of the company or the family. That was a very difficult transition, as once again the family was split.

The most recent hiring of a new CEO finally led to a good one! But it also produced problems. These days, only a few family members work for the company. We have 700 employees and only three full-time family employees. Because one of them is my brother, I hear from him what's going on from the perspective of the employees. But he isn't in top management; he and my cousin are just below the top. Their presence can be a little tricky because my cousin and I on the board hear from family members who work in the company, but the other two family board members do not have that link. That's one of the complexities of being in a family business.

DESIGNING A PROFESSIONAL BOARD

The board of directors is the core instrument for a family to build and sustain its distinctive culture and exercise values-based oversight. It upholds the legacy and values and defines the relationships among owners and across generations, and also remains open to anticipating and initiating change to take advantage of new possibilities or respond to crises.

Duties of board members

Because this is a family enterprise, the board has the added responsibility of considering the concerns of family members. The board needs to keep them informed about decisions and the reasons behind them while remaining mindful of the concerns, ideas, and values of all members of the family. Family members who serve on the board need to adopt a different mindset. Instead of looking out for their own family or branch, they now are asked to consider the needs of the entire family. A family member must be tutored in this ownership mindset before going onto the board

Board members are expected to be capable, competent, and committed to the entire business entity. They have the following duties:

- **Duty of Care:** diligence, staying informed, asking questions, attending meetings and reading Board materials.

- **Duty of Candor:** sharing concerns and observations truthfully even if they are difficult or unwelcome.

- **Duty of Loyalty:** showing undivided allegiance to the organization's welfare, avoiding conflicts of interest and making decisions in the best interest of the business while putting aside self-interest.

- **Duty of Obedience:** staying faithful to the organization's mission and avoiding taking any actions inconsistent with this mission.

RESILIENCE OF 100-YEAR FAMILY ENTERPRISES

Evolution of Boards

Boards develop over generations. They evolve from an informal group of owner/managers to include other family members, then non-family advisors, and finally family and non-family directors. By the third generation, most generative families have a board with both family and independent, non-family directors.

The board of a family enterprise evolves across generations in several steps:

The Stages of Board Development

1

Passive family membership representing branches

2

Board begins to engage and mediate different family interests

3

Family owners enlist professional advisors as a resource for development

4

Addition of non-family directors

5

Non-family board majority, especially if they are a public company

HOW OPPORTUNISTIC INNOVATION, BUSINESS DISCIPLINE, AND A CULTURE OF STEWARDSHIP GUIDE THE JOURNEY ACROSS GENERATIONS

Each family board has its own trajectory of development, as they respond to business and family challenges. This account illustrates this development in one family:

> As the second generation became older and started professions of their own, the board started to grow as well. But as the board grew, it had to deal with concerns about maintaining family values and practices. The second and third generations continued to add to these rules and structures. Philanthropies were often initiated by the third generation; they had a say because they were represented early on the board. They're looking now at the fourth generation to enforce and strengthen what they have been doing. There is even an idea that we could put together a junior board for high school and college kids, so they can prepare for these responsibilities.

> The board oversees everything: the company as well as internal family decisions. Most members of our family office board are also board members of public companies, so it's run like any other boardroom. In addition to making decisions about companies, investments, and structuring new divisions, they're also developing education for the next generation. So, it's very inclusive.

> The original criteria for being a board member was simply someone who achieved an executive level in the outside world. Those who came on the board at an early age were already accomplished in their fields. The most recent changes state that if you are responsible for a significant portion of the family's holdings, you should be on the board. Now, new family members are included as well.

Even though family shareholders may not have management roles, they can be involved in defining and sustaining the family culture as shown in this account:

> We are very involved in the business, though nobody in the family has an executive position. All family owners are on the board, and we have a board meeting every month. That's how we relate to the business. We are also involved with many other activities in the company. At the end of the year we do strategic planning for the next three years. Each company does its own strategic planning, but we are all very involved with what we call the Values and Vision Process.

Founders initially resist having formal boards; they see them as intruding on their control. They prefer informal advisors they can consult with confidentially. This works because they are only accountable to themselves. As new generations emerge, however, family owners and young future owners expect and even demand more transparency and clarity. They need to feel that ways exist to challenge the leaders and initiate necessary changes. Without this challenge, it would be much more difficult to achieve business discipline and strategic innovation.

Another account of board evolution came from this family:

> Until this April we only had family members. The third generation had six family lines— one son, and five daughters. Three sons-in-law and a grandson ran the business. Eventually those four turned into two leaders in the fourth generation. My father was the son of one of the sons-in-law in the business. Each family line had a seat on the board for 50 years or more. This policy of one board member per family line was an understanding from 1970. In 1999, we put in a fairly elaborate voting procedure and changed the bylaws; now, it's part of the bylaws that each family line gets a seat on the board.

> When we did that we also allowed for up to three additional, non-family directors. Since the 60s, the secretary/treasurer has always been non-family. The guy who was secretary/treasurer became the first non-family member on the board in 134 years.

RESILIENCE OF 100-YEAR FAMILY ENTERPRISES

In this family, a business challenge—new technology—precipitated a shift from family control to control by a professional board because they saw the need for experienced oversight by those with greater technical capability:

We transitioned from 100% family hands-on control and operation to a blend. The family maintained control over fundamental issues, but we created a board made up of family members and independent outsiders. This board provides critical business leadership and management that is a blend of family and non-family. We don't have an exact formula for this blend; over time it's shifted from more family to more independent outsiders.

FORMING THE BOARD

Because they are the central governing entities for the family enterprises, generative families spend a great deal of time considering how their boards are constituted. A good board must balance several factors, starting with the interests of the owners, both major and minor, other family members, and future owners. Then there is allocating the fruit of the enterprises; this includes the need for investment in innovation, development of business discipline, and returns to family owners. A good board needs to represent the owners, but it must also obtain professional expertise relevant to the current and future needs of the business.

Boards often have different categories of members. Commonly, boards select or elect a member from each family branch or constituency. By the third or fourth generation, the importance of branch identity declines. In addition, by this time most family boards develop a mechanism for selecting family members. Sometimes this is done by the board or the major family owners and sometimes by some sort of family election. If there is a private trust company, the board must contain a certain percentage of independent directors.

Families often have two classes of stock: voting and non-voting shares. This is done to preserve and focus authority over the business when there are many owners. A family often controls a public company without having majority ownership by having the voting shares held only by members of the family.

A family with two branches with a 60/40 share of ownership felt that having independent directors was the best way to protect the rights of the minority family branch. Another European family had six branches, each with a board seat and control of one of the family businesses. Then, as the fourth generation came on board, they overhauled the process, with an appointed board deciding whether business leaders should be family or non-family members.

Because of their personal relationships and family nature, some families, like this one, move away from one share one vote to other ways of voting that introduce more equality for family members:

The person with two shares has the same voice, the same questions, and gets the same attention as the person with 20,000 shares. I think I've been able to accomplish this because I come to it without much personal baggage. I'm very inclusionary. If you call me up with a list ten of questions and you own two shares, I'll answer your questions with the same vigor that I would if you had 20,000 shares. We don't see shares; we are a family.

HOW OPPORTUNISTIC INNOVATION, BUSINESS DISCIPLINE, AND A CULTURE OF STEWARDSHIP GUIDE THE JOURNEY ACROSS GENERATIONS

One model seen in large families with multiple businesses consists of a family holding company with family "managing directors" of individual business entities. This arrangement keeps family members from directly competing with each other. It also allows for diversity in managing individual businesses while creating alignment and integration at the whole family level. Here's how one family made this work:

> *There are now six family board members (this number can vary) who are also trustees of the trust. This includes three members from the fifth generation (Tim's dad, who is 64, and two uncles, 86 and 63 years old) and three from the sixth (Tim and two cousins, ages 45 and 49). Each of the 6 runs a division of the business. They are active owners. Tim would like to bring on an external advisor at some point. They meet formally once a year in July for 2 ½ days and informally when decisions need to be made. The six make decisions together.*

In other families, the businesses are more independent:

> *The business has become increasingly diversified over the generations. It's become almost a conglomerate at this point, and several families have exited. We had a liquidity event in 2006 to 2007 when we sold a manufacturing plant. We now have four contracting related businesses: agriculture and real estate partnerships and a couple of investment vehicles. We also have an ESOP (employee stock ownership plan) through the construction businesses. Each business has a separate board.*

Some families, especially older families outside of the US, limit ownership to the family members who work in the business. Other family members are compensated for their shares as in this example:

> *My brother, my cousin, and I share a certain personality and interest in adventure. We have this rule: you can only be a shareholder if you are active in the business. With that rule we avoid a situation where you have many shareholders who are there just to collect dividends. These shareholders might have a more conservative approach and say, "Let's conserve what we have. We don't need any new experiments or risk please. Dividends come before reinvestment." We've never had to deal with that kind of attitude because nobody can join who is not working in the business.*

As the business grows over generations, requirements for board members become more stringent. Each generation finds they must set the bar higher for board members. One family has a board with four family representatives, one from each branch. The board actively seeks and recruits good candidates, and these are not elected, but selected. The board is always looking for good future prospects.

Over time, families may get more explicit as they develop fair, transparent, and effective selection processes:

> *We have a formal process for electing family directors by the whole family. The family nominates the family director for the seat coming from the family side and then the whole family votes. This is not a one vote per share system, but rather one vote per family member, so every family member has a vote.*

To anticipate conflict, this family defines the criteria for selecting family board members:

> *We discussed guidelines for good board members with our next generation board members. What should a good board member study? What does he or she need to know? What kind of experience is expected? It's amazing how much energy was put into refusing to deal with this discussion. Many people didn't understand what it meant. They said, "How can anybody oblige the parents to put or not to put their kids on the board?" We answered, "Nobody is obliging you. We just want some guidelines for fourth gens to know what is expected.*

RESILIENCE OF 100-YEAR FAMILY ENTERPRISES

A board oversees the company, family office, and/or foundation. But in many cases, the family council chooses family board members for the owners. One family uses "back channels" to dialogue about who would be good nominees; this is sometimes contentious. The family council then interviews prospects and makes recommendations to the board.

In other cases, like the one described below, the family and board find ways to split the responsibility of appointing family board members:

> *The terms for the board of directors are basically one-year terms, but there's no term limit. There's an age limit of 70. Right now, we've got three family members on the board, and they're all going to turn 70 at the same time.*
>
> *When there's an opening, a letter goes out to the family, people apply, and the council interviews the candidates. It's a pretty structured process; a set of questions are sent to those who are interested. In addition, there's an interview process with the family council. After that, the council makes a recommendation to the board. The council does not choose the family director, but the board pays a lot of attention to the recommendation. So far, they have gone with our recommendation every time.*
>
> *The council is also very involved in selecting the CEO. They interview prospective CEO candidates and then their recommendation to the board. Recently, a family member and two non-family members were up for a position. The family council did not recommend the family member. That gave the board permission to decide for one of the non-family members. It was a 5-4 vote, but it ended up being absolutely the right decision. But If the council had said, "We really want this family member," I think that would've swayed the board in that direction.*

Another family had a unique dilemma. A highly qualified in-law was proposed for the board, but the family felt this person was not connected enough to the family; he didn't come to family reunions and didn't know what the family wanted. Both of these were expectations for board membership; it was not just a business decision. He was not selected. Instead, he was told that before he could serve, he would have to interact more with the family.

This family has one-year board terms, so they have to be re-elected every year:

> *Right now, we have a system for choosing board members, with deadlines and a formal evaluation committee. Everything is transparent and based on best practices. We're trying to head conflicts and encourage as much family involvement as possible.*

Another family with many shareholders has an elaborate process of checks and balances:

> *We have 135 family members and 87 shareholders, but we only have two people employed in the business. Five of our eleven directors are family members along with nine on the family council. Our policy is that anybody in the family can nominate a family member for the board of directors. The family council gathers those names and resumes and decides which individuals are qualified to be board members. We then send two or three names to the nominating committee.*
>
> *Since the 1950s, our policy has been that there will always be more outside directors on the board than family members. Outside directors interview family nominees and decide who will be on the board. This selection process avoids hard feelings among family members; for example, they can't accuse another member of vetoing their favorite candidate. It also allows the family to be free of an entitled mentality,*

as in, "I want to be a director and, therefore, I get to be a director." A director is a professional position and should be decided on merit. Having the outside directors make the final decision ensures that the most qualified people will be chosen.

In every family, young family members need to learn about the business, the role of the board, and skills are required for board membership. Membership is not a prize but a responsibility; it's a professional role. One family formed a **junior board** made up of family members who wanted to develop their skills and knowledge. Junior boards help the business to achieve transparency while teaching and preparing younger members for roles on the board. The junior boards also enable the family to recognize capability and develop it. Another family formed an **advisory board** comprised of family members who met with the board as learners and, occasionally, provided informal strategic advice. These informal **board observers** or advisors then became potential candidates for formal membership. Here's how this worked in one family:

A year ago, we decided it would be to our benefit to have more family members on the board. We thought this would encourage the education of more family members about the business and ensure that board decisions were aligned with the shareholder's values. At the time, there was only one family member on the board along with six nonfamily members. We decided we didn't want to replace any current members, so we added two more family members.

Assuming that my cousin and I become full board members, we'd then have three family members out of nine directors. We've learned that being a board member has a big learning curve, especially in this kind of technical business. It takes a long time to get up to speed to be useful, so we really don't want people rotating off that quickly.

When a strong leader died in a company, the successor wanted to develop the next generation. He selected not the oldest but the most qualified to sit on the board, and that caused some tension. Another family developed seven competencies required for a board member. The board solicits prospects via letter, and the candidate then states how well he or she fulfills the criteria. The board then selects the best candidate.

Another family had a discussion of board responsibility and structure, and then passed the baton as the old board resigned and a new one was installed. They went from two brothers to a board of eight, all of whom were well qualified for the position.

The earlier generations of leaders teach their heirs that board service is a responsibility, not a perk for family members:

I'm trying to inculcate the perspective of what it means to be a good owner. When I reflect on the problems of the past, we've always had sort of mixed management and ownership, and that's created a lot of fights. The idea that their responsibility is to be a good owner is fundamental to what we're trying to achieve. We're in the midst of developing a new approach in which the main task of the board of directors is to oversee the entire enterprise. We're looking at our businesses as a true portfolio and empowering separate boards for each underlying business. We have flexibility in shaping the portfolio for the future. This can also present opportunities for subsequent generations to be involved in the businesses in many different ways.

RESILIENCE OF 100-YEAR FAMILY ENTERPRISES

As generations pass, each new generation needs to learn their roles and responsibilities:

> We're trying to consider how to bring in the fifth and sixth generations. Board membership provides a forum for engagement and a way for stockholders to move to the idea of stewardship. Our challenge has been to define clear roles and boundaries between the family council, the board, and management. That's been tricky. When I first came on the board, our board and management were pretty antagonistic towards family stockholders. When I walked into my first board meeting, I was suddenly on the hot seat about something that involved my uncle; this was an awful experience. I realized that we needed new board members, but the current structure for electing them was not going to work. Most stockholders didn't even know who the outside directors were.

> We named an ad hoc **Board Selection and Election Taskforce** to develop a new structure for electing board members. They established term limits and considered a retirement age. Up to then, it was like being appointed to the Supreme Court: you had to die to have your seat open up. This process took two years. All the old directors got the message and resigned, so we didn't have to throw them out. We created a robust search committee, and now we have a great new board and CEO, and we are mostly on the same page. There are five family members on the board, if you include the CEO who has a seat.

One family member developed insight into the role by serving as an independent director of other family businesses:

> I am an independent director on the board of two family businesses; I do this because I want to support the family in protecting their wealth. I also want to listen to the things they want. I feel that I can do this better than family members who are owners of these businesses because I'm not involved emotionally; I can make impartial decisions.

Independent Board Members.

The inclusion of independent board directors is part of an overall transformation of the family enterprise, as illustrated here:

> We created a board last year that includes outsiders. We are integrating all of our companies under a single board and CEO. We approved our new structure in 2013 and named two co-chairs—two of my cousins—to guide us through the transition. For the first time in our history, we hired a non-family CEO. We wanted our cousins to work side by side with the new CEO for the first six months to make sure he learns everything and can take full advantage of their support. Then they will relinquish all operative functions and the CEO will be fully in control.

Over generations, generative families tended to increase the number of independent directors:

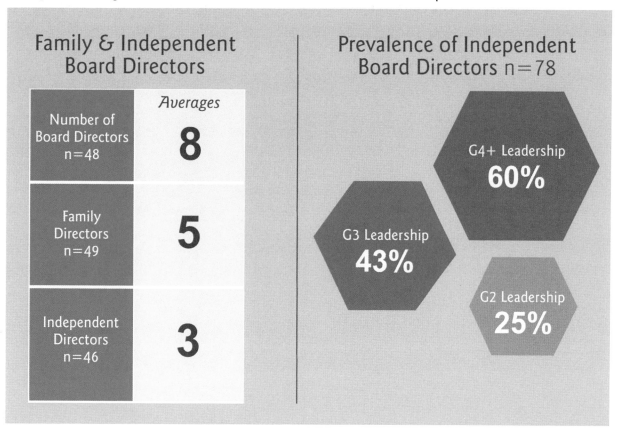

Families have different ratios of family directors and independent directors. Some have a family majority, others do not. One board of 11 contained three family members, reduced from four. Most of our families have several independent directors, with some having an independent majority.

When independent board members are appointed, the family faces a challenge: Should the family be committed to implementing good ideas suggested by the new, independent board members? Suppose they suggest an idea that makes good business sense but doesn't have the support of the family? One family that had a majority of independent members solved this problem by requiring every decision to have at least one family member in agreement.

In this family, the widows of the second-generation siblings transitioned to a professional third generation that included several independent board members:

> *Our purpose in having a private trust company is to manage the diversification of the family's wealth rather than leaving it up to the institutional trustees who may not know us. We recruited our first group of independent board members, and this allowed us to retire my aunts from the board of directors (they were well meaning, but not well versed in business strategy). After the independent board was in place, two things happened. First, the independent board asked me to become president and chief operating officer. Second, they suggested we put forward the [tender] offer to enable those members of the family who were unhappy with the changes to liquidate some of their ownership. We ended up purchasing 57% of the equity of the company.*

We can see that governance is the unifying and integrating process that sustains the generative stakeholder alliance—and that this, in turn, sustains the long-term family enterprise. Having an active board that acts as stewards and contains independent directors and competent representatives of family owners allows the family to focus on the business goals of craftsmanship and innovation. Business governance is the ringmaster of family organization and continuity.

HOW OPPORTUNISTIC INNOVATION, BUSINESS DISCIPLINE, AND A CULTURE OF STEWARDSHIP GUIDE THE JOURNEY ACROSS GENERATIONS

Taking Action In Your Own Family Enterprise

Evolving Governance

This section outlined the developmental arc of business governance for a family enterprise. You can conduct an audit of the state of your own family governance to see how far along you are. The key is to develop the appropriate governance process to fit your current state and anticipate and prepare for the next generation. At each point in time, you should consider the approaching challenges in your family and in the business and then begin to develop a structure that fits where you are going, not just where you are.

You can look at where you are right now along the developmental arc of board/governance development and see what will be needed to serve you in the near future.

GOVERNANCE/ BOARD QUALITY	HAVE NOW?	HOW THIS MIGHT BE USEFUL	WHAT WE MIGHT NEED SOON?
Insiders Board– Owner/Operators			
Board With All Major Family Owners			
Board With Representative Family Owners			
Cross-Generational Representation On Board			
Non-Family Advisors To Board			
Independent Board Members			
Independent Board Member Majority			

Next, you can consider how the family is engaged in business governance by answering these questions:

- How transparent to family members are the operations of the business and the changes that are being considered?

- How are the growing members of the rising generation informed about the business?

- How are young and inexperienced family members educated about what is happening?

- How are family ideas and input about business policy accessed and listened to?

- How can new family members become involved in governance?

- How visible are the qualifications and selection of board members?

Part Six – Will There Be Another Generation?

The family enterprise is a core social building block for a civil society. In an impersonal world, the family enterprise is based on human relationships and values translated to fit the world of commerce, adding necessary humanity to the sterile landscape of commerce. Enduring family enterprises add strength, consistency, caring and sustained productivity to the economies of every nation. Because of this, their experiences are valuable to public, non-family enterprises.

The generative, multi-generational families that we studied offer a model of wealth creation that diverges from the conventional model of pursuit of self-interest, exclusive focus on profits and aggressive competition. Business families play the game of private enterprise well. But they grow and remain profitable within a values-based legacy that links their success to the success of others. This model has a lot to teach to public, non-family businesses.

But a family enterprise can't last forever. Though it can stem the tide of dissolution over a handful of generations, over time the extended family becomes too large to sustain as a unified entity. It then breaks up into smaller family or household units or distributes its wealth so that each individual can create his or her own future.

Nevertheless, when we look for long-lived businesses, we find that the global terrain consists mostly of family enterprises. Many qualities are incredibly unique and important about them and contrast their development with non-family companies. With a family at the helm, the enterprise can sustain a vision and values even as it continually takes new forms and develops new generations of leadership. As value-based enterprises, they are able to look not just at profitability but also at social goals. Because they look to the long-term future and have the ability to reinvest resources, it is not uncommon for the family to consider the kind of future they desire in their community and the world and use their enterprise to help bring about this vision.

Our research documents the many contributions of these families beyond commercial success. They have a deep impact in the community and on their loyal and long-term employees, suppliers and customers. Their family nature leads them to stand for something enduring, excellent and positive that is widely respected. They are values-based, and their values are often as important as profits.

Much media attention has been focused on the effects of wealth on young people, who are presented as excessive consumers of luxury goods, and entitled young people not respecting the needs or values of others. In our interviews and observations of the rising generations of generative families, we see more evidence of teaching, modeling and passing on values of responsibility, caring and respect for others, and contributing rather than consuming. Sustaining family wealth includes restraint in consumption as well as business growth. The ways that young family members add value, innovate, and become competent professionals in their families offers a more positive view of inherited wealth.

Moving Your Own Family Enterprise Toward Generativity

Here's a brief review of the goals and aspirations of generative family businesses and the means by which they accomplish these goals:

I. How to maintain the family business as a successful enterprise:

● Separate family from business concerns and work effectively in each area.

● Hire professional, non-family leaders. This usually happens by the third generation.

● Set strict conditions for family members wanting to work in the company.

● Reinvest in the company instead of taking short-term profits.

● Consider the long-term future when making decisions.

● Leaders able to let go and rethink what they are doing.

● Maintain openness to new ideas and strategies.

2. How to sustain the family vision and values in the business:

● Hire professionals who understand the family values.

● Form a family council or similar group to guide the leaders and maintain family values.

● Instill the family's values in the rising generations.

● Consider all stakeholders: family, employees, shareholders, customers, and community.

● Include impact on the nation and the world when making business decisions.

3. How to maintain family interest in the business:

● Maintain transparency in the operations of the business.

● Offer opportunity and pathways to involvement for each new generation.

● Create family camps and junior boards of directors to engage younger members. Some families hold family camps for young people in the summer. Others maintain junior boards of directors in which the younger members can learn about the workings of the company.

● Hold annual meetings. Many generative families hold annual meetings where the members learn what the business has been doing and discuss issues for the future.

RESILIENCE OF 100-YEAR FAMILY ENTERPRISES

The companies covered in this paper are extremely successful enterprises, still profitable and growing over many generations. Ironically, they have arrived at this success not by focusing on short-term profits but by maintaining a long-term outlook coupled with concern for all the company's stakeholders. This stands in sharp contrast to the current emphasis on increasing profits and raising the price of a firm's stock by whatever means possible.

Do we expect that the generative families in our study will continue for further generations? Our impression is that while they have been highly successful for three or more generations, many of the families in our study are not likely to survive as unified family entities for more than another generation. As they grow in numbers, the pressure for different paths leads and the sheer number of owners, leads them to break down into smaller units. Individual households will exit, and businesses will be sold. There are many opportunities for the family to consider different directions, and we think the media have made a mistake to portray businesses that sell or separate as failures. A huge portfolio of businesses that offers hundreds of family descendants a legacy of values, support for personal development, a wonderful shared history, and an opportunity to make their own contribution and forge their own path cannot be seen as a failure in any way. The generative family enterprise is a choice made by some unique and dedicated families, that is not right for many others.

This working paper and the others that report on our research into generative families, offer many insights to families in early stages of their own business. The wisdom of the generative family can also be used by non-family businesses. While most businesses are not family owned, it's possible to create a "family feeling" among managers and employees. This can occur when employees feel that they are treated fairly and included in the decision-making process. Family enterprises make a habit of getting input from as many family members—and other stakeholders—as possible. This custom can also be adopted by non-family businesses. While they may not have family members, they can get input from just as many other stakeholders.

We hope that the business evolution and stories of these very rare, special and unique family enterprises has enriched our understanding of how business can survive and thrive over many generations.

Acknowledgements

This research paper and the 100-Year Family Enterprise Project is a community effort with many participants.

Research Team. A wonderful group of professionals who have conducted the interviews and acted as a support group for this project and each other. This team includes Peter Begalla, Emily Bouchard, Jane Flanagan, James Grubman, Charlotte Lamp, Isabelle Lescent-Giles, Susan Massenzio, Joshua Nacht, Michael O'Neal, Jamie Trager-Muney, and Keith Whitaker.

Charlotte Lamp recorded the demographic information, and Jane Flanagan created the charts.

Janet Schatzman created the graphics. Sam Case helped with the editing.

Merrill Lynch. Next is Merrill Lynch's Center for Family Wealth Dynamics and Governance® (Center) and Merrill Lynch's Family Office Services who generously sponsored this paper and the previous working paper. Specifically, I'd like to acknowledge Matthew Wesley, a director of the Center based in Seattle; Stacy Allred, managing director and head of the Center; and Valerie Galinskaya, a director of the Center based in New York; who supported and offered valuable input and advice in developing this paper. Additionally, I enjoyed collaborating with the Center team to develop their own working paper, inspired by this research.

U.S. Trust, Bank of America Private Wealth Management. Next is U.S. Trust, Bank of America Private Wealth Management, who served as a co-sponsor along with Merrill Lynch's Center for Family Wealth Dynamics and Governance® and Merrill Lynch's Family Office Services. Specifically, I'd like to thank Peter Hillsman, Karen Reynolds Sharkey and Howard Weiss, who provided input.

About Wise Counsel Research

Wise Counsel Research is an award-winning charitable think-tank founded in 2008. It produces educational resources on family enterprise, philanthropy, and wealth. Publications include the 100-Year Family Study white papers, Cycle of the Gift (2012), Voice of the Rising Generation (2013), Family Trusts (2015), and Complete Family Wealth (2018). The associates of Wise Counsel Research are some of the leading researchers and practitioners in the field of family enterprise, including Dr. Dennis Jaffe, James "Jay" Hughes, Mary Duke, Peter Evans, Hartley Goldstone, Dr. Susan Massenzio, Rev. Scotty McLennan, Christian Stewart, and Dr. Keith Whitaker. In 2017 Wise Counsel Research was honored by Family Wealth Report for "outstanding contribution to wealth management thought-leadership." As a 501(c)3 public charity, gifts to Wise Counsel Research are fully deductible for state and federal income tax purposes; they also qualify for distributions from private foundations, donor-advised funds, and other planned giving vehicles.

About Merrill Lynch

The Center for Family Wealth Dynamics and Governance® at Merrill Lynch works collaboratively with wealthy individuals, their families and their advisors to empower families to define the purpose of their wealth and to be intentional about the impact of their wealth on themselves, their family and their community. Significant wealth brings substantial complexity. The Center exists to help families make sense of that complexity and find ways to thoughtfully navigate wealth in each generation to build individual and collective well-being, purpose and productivity. The Center helps families find the path that works for them, applying insights from research and its experience working with a multitude of significant families.

Merrill Lynch Family Office Services provides ultra-high-net worth families with highly sophisticated solutions designed to manage the complexities of substantial wealth. Family Office Principals work closely with each family, their Merrill Lynch Advisor, accountants, attorneys and other advisors to seamlessly implement a comprehensive approach that encompasses the family's overall financial, lifestyle and legacy goals and values. Merrill Lynch Family Office Services becomes a family's essential coordinator, counselor and support staff, delivering a streamlined experience allowing them to pursue personal aspirations knowing that experienced, dedicated professionals are focused on their affairs.

About U.S. Trust, Bank of America Private Wealth Management

For more than 200 years, through evolving markets, changing legal environments and the growing complexity of the financial world, U.S. Trust has helped clients manage wealth by providing disciplined financial strategies and a bridge between generations. Today, drawing on the strengths of Bank of America, we offer the benefits of broader reach and resources backed by our fiduciary[13] responsibility and commitment to personalized solutions.

Each client's unique financial opportunities, challenges and goals drive their relationships at U.S. Trust. Whether the objective is managing assets for increased cash flow, establishing and administering a trust, or growing and preserving wealth for future generations, clients can expect access to extensive resources and personalized solutions with the experience of a boutique private bank.

HOW OPPORTUNISTIC INNOVATION, BUSINESS DISCIPLINE, AND A CULTURE OF STEWARDSHIP GUIDE THE JOURNEY ACROSS GENERATIONS

About the Author: Dennis T. Jaffe, Ph.D.

For over 40 years, Dr. Dennis Jaffe has been one of the leading architects of the field of family enterprise consulting. As both an organizational consultant and clinical psychologist, he helps multi-generational families to develop governance practices that build the capability of next generation leadership and ensure ongoing capability of financial organizations and family offices to serve their family clients.

Dennis's work with families helps inform his training of financial advisors and wealth managers about the knowledge and skills needed to serve their client families. He is an acclaimed speaker and workshop leader in programs for business families and financial service firms.

Education and Professional Background

For 35 years, Dennis was professor of Organizational Systems and Psychology at Saybrook University in San Francisco, where he is now professor emeritus. He received his B.A. in Philosophy, M.A. in Management and Ph.D. in Sociology from Yale University.

Publications and Tools

His books guide business families in working together to build a great family and a thriving set of family enterprises. They include

- **Cross Cultures: How Global Families Negotiate Change Across Generations** (co-authored with James Grubman),

- **Stewardship of Your Family Enterprise: Developing Responsible Leadership Across Generations,** and

- **Working with the Ones You Love.**

He is the creator of several widely-used tools to help families learn about themselves and constructively grow across generations. **The Values Edge** uses a deck of cards to help individuals and families create personal and organizational values pyramids. The on-line **Family Enterprise Assessment Tool** enables multi-generational business families to understand the current status of their family dynamics and enterprise and explore their areas of difference.

Current Activities

As a member of **Wise Counsel Research Associates**, Dennis is now in third phase of his 100-Year Family Enterprise research project, resulting so far in three working papers (all available on Amazon)

- **Releasing the Potential of the Rising Generation,**

- **Good Fortune: Building a Hundred Year Family Enterprise,**

- **Governing the Family Enterprise,** and

- **Best Practices of Successful, Global, Multi-Generational Family Enterprises.**

His global insights have led to teaching or consulting engagements at Hult University in Dubai, the Pacific Asia chapter of Family Business Network, and the Advisory Board of Chinese University of Hong Kong. He is part of the Polaris team working with the Family Business Network to create a roadmap for family and business sustainability.

Previous Activities

He has been an active member of the Family Firm Institute since its inception, presenting at annual conferences, serving on the board, designing and delivering educational courses in their GEN program and writing for the Family Business Review. In honor of his achievements, Dennis was recognized with the prestigious Richard Beckhard Award for his contributions to FFI and the field.

He was also named Thinker in Residence in 2007 for South Australia, helping the region design a strategic plan for the future of Australian entrepreneurial and family businesses. He was the researcher for the JP Morgan 2005 study of best practices of multi-generational families, and a more recent study of succession in Asian families. In 2010 he was a visiting professor at the undergraduate family business program of Stetson University.

Dennis has been a frequent contributor to periodicals such as Family Business, Journal of Financial Planning, Private Wealth, Journal of Wealth Management, and Worth magazine. His work has been featured in Inc., NPR Marketplace, Entrepreneur, Time and The Wall Street Journal, and he was profiled in People Magazine. In 2005 he received the Editor's Choice Award from the Journal of Financial Planning for his article on family business strategic planning.

Active in nonprofit governance, he served on the boards of the World Business Academy, Saybrook University, and the Center for Mind-Body Medicine.

Pioneering Work in Values-Based Organizations and Holistic Health

As a founder and contributor to the field of organizational transformation and change leadership, Dennis co-authored a dozen influential management books, including **Getting Your Organization to Change, Rekindling Commitment**, and **Take this Job and Love It!** As founder of **Changeworks Global**, he guided organizations and family businesses to long-term change by unleashing the power of their employees. His research on the governance of start-up companies, *After the Term Sheet* is an important contribution to the field of entrepreneurship. He is co-creator of **Mastering the Transition Curve, StressMap**, and other tools that support personal and organizational success.

For three years, Dennis was co-editor of **The Inner Edge**, a magazine focused on spirituality in business. He was deputy director for research at the Macarthur Foundation sponsored Healthy Companies Network from 1992-95. As co-founder of the web firm MemeStreams, he pioneered on-line executive development tools. The video **Managing People through Change** was voted one of the Best Products of 1991 by Human Resource Executive. In the 70s, his holistic health books, From **Burnout to Balance** (retitled and reissued as **Self-Renewal**), and **Healing From Within**, were each honored with the Medical Self-Care Book Award. He was co-author of the international bestseller, **TM: Discovering Inner Energy and Overcoming Stress.**

Dennis lives in San Francisco, CA.   His website is **www.dennisjaffe.com**.

HOW OPPORTUNISTIC INNOVATION, BUSINESS DISCIPLINE, AND A CULTURE OF STEWARDSHIP GUIDE THE JOURNEY ACROSS GENERATIONS

Copies of this working paper are available in print and electronic versions from Amazon.

You can also purchase copies of our other working papers in this series:

- **Good Fortune: Building a Hundred Year Family Enterprise** (2013), an overview of the evolution of these families over generations.

- **Releasing the Potential of the Rising Generation: How Long-Lasting Family Enterprises Prepare Their Successors** (2016), details the activities design by families to develop their human capital across generations.

- **Governing the Family Enterprise: The Evolution of Family Councils, Assemblies and Constitutions** (2017) explores how the family develops governance for its non-business and financial activities.

- **Three Pathways to Evolutionary Survival: Best Practices of Successful, Global, Multi-Generational Family Enterprises** (2012), presents survey data from 200 families.

For print copies of this report, please contact:

Wise Counsel Research 76 Canton Avenue, Milton MA 02186

www.wisecounselresearch.com

To contact Dennis Jaffe for inquiries, questions and speaking and workshop events:
dennis@wisecounselresearch.com

Made in the USA
Coppell, TX
16 October 2020